MW0051O676

TO

_____

FROM

_____

TEENS

5 MINUTES A DAY

100 DEVOTIONS FOR GUYS

The quoted ideas expressed in this book (but not Scripture verses) are not, in all cases, exact quotations, as some have been edited for clarity and brevity. In all cases, the author has attempted to maintain the speaker's original intent. In some cases, quoted material for this book was obtained from secondary sources, primarily print media. While every effort was made to ensure the accuracy of these sources, the accuracy cannot be guaranteed. For additions, deletions, corrections, or clarifications in future editions of this text, please write Freeman-Smith, LLC.

Scripture quotations are taken from:

The Holy Bible, King James Version

The Holy Bible, New International Version (NIV) Copyright © 1973, 1978, 1984, by International Bible Society. Used by permission of Zondervan Publishing House. All rights reserved.

The Holy Bible, New King James Version (NKJV) Copyright © 1982 by Thomas Nelson, Inc. Used by permission.

The New American Standard Bible®, (NASB) Copyright © 1960, 1962, 1963, 1968, 1971, 1972, 1973, 1975, 1977, 1995 by The Lockman Foundation. Used by permission.

Holy Bible, New Living Translation, (NLT)copyright © 1996. Used by permission of Tyndale House Publishers, Inc., Wheaton, Illinois 60189. All rights reserved.

The Message (MSG)- This edition issued by contractual arrangement with NavPress, a division of The Navigators, U.S.A. Originally published by NavPress in English as THE MESSAGE: The Bible in Contemporary Language copyright 2002-2003 by Eugene Peterson. All rights reserved.

New Century Version®. (NCV) Copyright © 1987, 1988, 1991 by Word Publishing, a division of Thomas Nelson, Inc. All rights reserved. Used by permission.

The Holman Christian Standard Bible™ (HCSB) Copyright © 1999, 2000, 2001 by Holman Bible Publishers. Used by permission.

Cover Design by Kim Russell / Wahoo Designs

Page Layout by Bart Dawson

ISBN 978-160587-126-4

Printed in the United States of America

TEENS

100 DEVOTIONS FOR GUYS

But God demonstrates
his own love for us in this:
While we were still sinners,
Christ died for us.

—

ROMANS 5:8 NIV

Introduction

Okay, it's a fact: you're a very busy guy. But here's a question: can you squeeze five little minutes into your hectic schedule? If you're smart, the answer will be a resounding yes. Why? Because the five minutes in question are the minutes that you give to God!

God has a plan for everything, and that includes you. But figuring out that plan may not be easy. That's why you need to talk to God . . . a lot. The more you talk to your Creator, the sooner He will help you figure out exactly what plans He has in store for you. So do yourself a favor: start talking to Him now. As you begin that conversation, this little book can help.

This book contains 100 short devotional readings of particular interest to guys who, like you, are very busy. Each chapter contains Bible verses, a brief devotional reading, quotations from noted Christian men (plus quotes from a few women tossed in for good measure), and a prayer.

Would you like to have a life that's above and beyond the ordinary? Talk to God about it. Do you have questions that you can't answer? God has answers. Are you seeking to improve some aspect of your life? The Bible is the greatest self-improvement book of all time. Do you want to be a better person and a better Christian? If so, ask for God's help and ask for it many times each day . . . starting with a regular, heartfelt morning devotional. Even five minutes is enough time to change your day . . . and your life.

Who's First?

*The thing you should want most is God's kingdom
and doing what God wants. Then all these other things
you need will be given to you.*

MATTHEW 6:33 NCV

Who is in charge of your heart? Is it God, or is it something else? Have you given Christ your heart, your soul, your talents, your time, and your testimony? Or are you giving Him little more than a few hours each Sunday morning?

In the book of Exodus, God warns that we should place no gods before Him. Yet all too often, we place our Lord in second, third, or fourth place as we worship other things. When we unwittingly place possessions or relationships above our love for the Creator, we create big problems for ourselves.

Does God rule your heart? Make certain that the honest answer to this question is a resounding yes. In the life of every radical believer, God comes first. And that's precisely the place that He deserves in your heart.

God calls us to be committed to Him, to be committed to making a difference, and to be committed to reconciliation.

BILL HYBELS

God is able to do anything He pleases with one ordinary person fully consecrated to Him.

HENRY BLACKABY AND CLAUDE KING

We become whatever we are committed to.

RICK WARREN

Be careful not to forget the Lord.

DEUTERONOMY 6:12 HOLMAN CSB

It is good to give thanks to the Lord,
And to sing praises to Your name, O Most High;
To declare Your lovingkindness in the morning,
And Your faithfulness every night.

PSALM 92:1-2 NKJV

Love the Lord your God with all your heart,
with all your soul, and with all your strength.

DEUTERONOMY 6:5 HOLMAN CSB

Today's Prayer

Dear Lord, today I will honor You with
my thoughts, my actions, and my prayers.
I will seek to please You, and I will strive to
serve You. Your blessings are as limitless as
Your love. And because I have been so richly
blessed, I will worship You, Father, with
thanksgiving in my heart and praise
on my lips, this day and forever.

Amen

Devo 2

The Book He Wrote

*You will be a good servant of Christ Jesus,
constantly nourished on the words of the faith and
of the sound doctrine which you have been following.*
1 Timothy 4:6 NASB

I f you want to know God, you should read the book He
wrote. It's called the Bible, and it is one of the most
important tools that God uses to direct your steps and
transform your life.

As you seek to build a deeper relationship with your
Creator, you must decide whether God's Word will be a
bright spotlight that guides your path every day or a tiny
nightlight that occasionally flickers in the dark. The decision
to study the Bible—or not—is yours and yours alone. But
make no mistake: the way that you choose to use your Bible
will have a profound impact on you and your loved ones.

The Bible is unlike any other book. It is a priceless gift
from your Creator, a tool that God intends for you to use
in every aspect of your life. And, it contains promises upon
which you, as a Christian, can and must depend.

Reading news without reading the Bible will inevitably
lead to an unbalanced life, an anxious spirit,
a worried and depressed soul.

BILL BRIGHT

Try to get saturated with the gospel.

C. H. SPURGEON

God gives us a compass and a Book of promises and
principles—the Bible—and lets us make our decisions
day by day as we sense the leading of His Spirit.
This is how we grow.

WARREN WIERSBE

Blessed are those who hunger and thirst for righteousness,
for they will be filled.

MATTHEW 5:6 NIV

For the word of God is quick, and powerful, and sharper than
any two-edged sword, piercing even to the dividing asunder
of soul and spirit, and of the joints and marrow,
and is a discerner of the thoughts and intents of the heart.

HEBREWS 4:12 KJV

Jesus answered and said unto him,
If a man love me, he will keep my words:
and my Father will love him,
and we will come unto him,
and make our abode with him.

—

JOHN 14:23 KJV

Today's Prayer

Heavenly Father, Your Word is a light
unto the world; I will study it and trust it
and share it. In all that I do, help me be
a worthy witness for You as I share
the Good News of Your perfect Son
and Your perfect Word.
Amen

Devo 3

It's a Wonderful Life

For whoever finds me finds life
and receives favor from the LORD.
PROVERBS 8:35 NIV

Life can be tough sometimes, but it's also wonderful—and it's a glorious gift from God. How will you use that gift? Will you treat this day as a precious treasure from your Heavenly Father, or will you take the next 24 hours for granted? The answer should be obvious: Every day, including this one, comes gift-wrapped from God—your job is to unwrap that gift, to use it wisely, and to give thanks to the Giver.

Instead of sleepwalking through life, you must wake up and live in the precious present. Each waking moment holds the potential to celebrate, to serve, to share, or to love. Because you are a person with incalculable potential, each moment has incalculable value. Your challenge is to experience each day to the fullest as you seek to live in accordance with God's plan for your life. When you do, you'll experience His abundance and His peace.

Are you willing to treat this day (and every one hereafter) as a special gift to be savored and celebrated? You should—and if you seek to Live with a capital L, you most certainly will.

Life is a glorious opportunity.

BILLY GRAHAM

You've heard the saying, "Life is what you make it."
That means we have a choice. We can choose to have
a life full of frustration and fear, but we can just as easily
choose one of joy and contentment.

DENNIS SWANBERG

People, places, and things were never meant to give us life.
God alone is the author of a fulfilling life.

GARY SMALLEY & JOHN TRENT

*Make it your ambition to lead a quiet life, to mind your own
business and to work with your hands, just as we told you,
so that your daily life may win the respect of outsiders
and so that you will not be dependent on anybody.*

1 THESSALONIANS 4:11-12 NIV

*I came so they can have real and eternal life,
more and better life than they ever dreamed of.*

JOHN 10:10 MSG

I urge you to live a life worthy
of the calling you have received.

—

EPHESIANS 4:1 NIV

Today's Prayer

Dear Lord, You have created this glorious universe, and You have created me. Let me live my life to the fullest, and let me use my life for Your glory, today and every day.

Amen

Devo 4

The Good News

*Grace to you and peace from God our Father
and the Lord Jesus Christ.*
PHILIPPIANS 1:2 NASB

Here's the great news: God's grace is not earned . . . and thank goodness it's not! If God's grace were some sort of reward for good behavior, none of us could earn enough brownie points to win the big prize. But it doesn't work that way. Grace is a free offer from God. By accepting that offer, we transform our lives today and forever.

God's grace is not just any old gift; it's the ultimate gift, and we owe Him our eternal gratitude. Our Heavenly Father is waiting patiently for each of us to accept His Son and receive His grace. Let us accept that gift today so that we might enjoy God's presence now and throughout all eternity.

The grace of God is infinite and eternal.
As it had no beginning, so it can have no end, and being
an attribute of God, it is as boundless as infinitude.

A. W. TOZER

The grace of God is sufficient for all our needs,
for every problem, and for every difficulty, for every
broken heart, and for every human sorrow.

PETER MARSHALL

You don't earn grace, and you don't deserve grace;
you simply receive it as God's loving gift,
and then share it with others.

WARREN WIERSBE

*For by grace you are saved through faith,
and this is not from yourselves; it is God's gift
not from works, so that no one can boast.*

EPHESIANS 2:8-9 HOLMAN CSB

*And we have seen and testify that the Father has sent
the Son as Savior of the world.*

1 JOHN 4:14 NKJV

FOR GUYS

My grace is sufficient for you,
for My strength is made perfect
in weakness.

—

2 Corinthians 12:9 NKJV

Today's Prayer

Lord, You have saved me by Your grace. Keep me mindful that Your grace is a gift that I can accept but cannot earn. I praise You for that priceless gift, today and forever. Let me share the good news of Your grace with a world that desperately needs Your healing touch.

Amen

Devo 5

Doing the Right Thing

Lead a tranquil and quiet life in all godliness and dignity.
1 TIMOTHY 2:2 HOLMAN CSB

Okay pal, answer this question honestly: Do you behave differently because of your relationship with Jesus? Or do you behave in pretty much the same way that you would if you weren't a believer? Hopefully, the fact that you've invited Christ to reign over your heart means that you've made BIG changes in your thoughts and your actions.

Doing the right thing is not always easy, especially when you're tired or frustrated. But, doing the wrong thing almost always leads to trouble. And sometimes, it leads to BIG trouble.

If you're determined to follow "the crowd," you may soon find yourself headed in the wrong direction. So here's some advice: Don't follow the crowd—follow Jesus. And keep following Him every day of your life, beginning with this day.

The purity of motive determines the quality of action.

OSWALD CHAMBERS

The best evidence of our having the truth is
our walking in the truth.

MATTHEW HENRY

If we have the true love of God in our hearts,
we will show it in our lives. We will not have to go up
and down the earth proclaiming it.
We will show it in everything we say or do.

D. L. MOODY

*Therefore as you have received Christ Jesus the Lord,
walk in Him.*

COLOSSIANS 2:6 HOLMAN CSB

*Who is wise and understanding among you?
He should show his works by good conduct
with wisdom's gentleness.*

JAMES 3:13 HOLMAN CSB

So don't get tired of doing what is good.
Don't get discouraged and give up,
for we will reap a harvest of blessing
at the appropriate time.

—

GALATIANS 6:9 NLT

Today's Prayer

Lord, there is a right way and a wrong way to
live. Let me live according to Your rules,
not the world's rules. Your path is right for me,
God; let me follow it every day of my life.
Amen

Devo 6

Your Bright Future

What a God we have! And how fortunate we are to have him, this Father of our Master Jesus! Because Jesus was raised from the dead, we've been given a brand-new life and have everything to live for, including a future in heaven—and the future starts now!

1 PETER 1:3-4 MSG

How bright is your future? Well, if you're a faithful believer, God's plans for you are so bright that you'd better wear shades. But here's an important question: How bright do you believe your future to be? Are you expecting a terrific tomorrow, or are you dreading a terrible one? The answer you give will have a powerful impact on the way tomorrow turns out.

Do you trust in the ultimate goodness of God's plan for your life? Will you face tomorrow's challenges with optimism and hope? You should. After all, God created you for a very important reason: His reason. And you still have important work to do: His work.

Today, as you live in the present and look to the future, remember that God has an amazing plan for you. Act—and believe—accordingly.

The Christian believes in a fabulous future.

BILLY GRAHAM

Hoping for a good future without investing in today is like a farmer waiting for a crop without ever planting any seed.

JOHN MAXWELL

The pages of your past cannot be rewritten, but the pages of your tomorrows are blank.

ZIG ZIGLAR

Do not boast about tomorrow, for you do not know what a day may bring forth.

PROVERBS 27:1 NKJV

For now we see indistinctly, as in a mirror, but then face to face. Now I know in part, but then I will know fully, as I am fully known.

1 CORINTHIANS 13:12 HOLMAN CSB

Today's Prayer

Dear Lord, as I look to the future, I will place my trust in You. If I become discouraged, I will turn to You. If I am afraid, I will seek strength in You. You are my Father, and I will place my hope, my trust, and my faith in You.

Amen

Devo 7

What Kind of Example?

*You should be an example to the believers in speech,
in conduct, in love, in faith, in purity.*

1 TIMOTHY 4:12 HOLMAN CSB

Okay, here's a question: What kind of example are you? Are you the kind of guy whose life serves as a powerful example of decency and morality? Are you a guy whose behavior serves as a positive role model for others? Are you the kind of guy whose actions, day in and day out, are based upon integrity, fidelity, and a love for the Lord? If so, you are not only blessed by God, you are also a powerful force for good in a world that desperately needs positive influences such as yours.

Phillips Brooks advised, "Be such a man, and live such a life, that if every man were such as you, and every life a life like yours, this earth would be God's Paradise." And that's sound advice because our families and friends are watching . . . and so, for that matter, is God.

In our faith we follow in someone's steps.
In our faith we leave footprints to guide others.
It's the principle of discipleship.

MAX LUCADO

We urgently need people who encourage
and inspire us to move toward God and away
from the world's enticing pleasures.

JIM CYMBALA

A holy life will produce the deepest impression.
Lighthouses blow no horns; they only shine.

D. L. MOODY

*Do everything without grumbling and arguing,
so that you may be blameless and pure.*

PHILIPPIANS 2:14–15 HOLMAN CSB

*Set an example of good works yourself,
with integrity and dignity in your teaching.*

TITUS 2:7 HOLMAN CSB

Test all things; hold fast what is good.
Abstain from every form of evil.

—

1 Thessalonians 5:21-22 NKJV

Today's Prayer

Lord, make me a worthy example to my family and friends. And, let my words and my deeds serve as a testimony to the changes You have made in my life. Let me praise You, Father, by following in the footsteps of Your Son, and let others see Him through me.

Amen

Devo 8

Kindness Is a Choice

A kind man benefits himself,
but a cruel man brings disaster on himself.
PROVERBS 11:17 HOLMAN CSB

Kindness is a choice. Sometimes, when we feel happy or generous, we find it easy to be kind. Other times, when we are discouraged or tired, we can scarcely summon the energy to utter a single kind word. But, God's commandment is clear: He intends that we make the conscious choice to treat others with kindness and respect, no matter our circumstances, no matter our emotions.

In the busyness and confusion of daily life, it is easy to lose focus, and it is easy to become frustrated. We are imperfect human beings struggling to manage our lives as best we can, but we often fall short. When we are distracted or disappointed, we may neglect to share a kind word or a kind deed. This oversight hurts others, but it hurts us most of all.

Today, slow yourself down and be alert for people who need your smile, your kind words, or your helping hand. Make kindness a centerpiece of your dealings with others. They will be blessed, and you will be too.

Do all the good you can. By all the means you can.
In all the ways you can. In all the places you can.
At all the times you can. To all the people you can.
As long as ever you can.

JOHN WESLEY

Be so preoccupied with good will that
you haven't room for ill will.

E. STANLEY JONES

When you extend hospitality to others, you're not trying to
impress people, you're trying to reflect God to them.

MAX LUCADO

Love is patient; love is kind.
1 CORINTHIANS 13:4 HOLMAN CSB

*And may the Lord make you increase
and abound in love to one another and to all.*
1 THESSALONIANS 3:12 NKJV

Today's Prayer

Help me, Lord, to see the needs of those around me. Today, let me show courtesy to those who cross my path. Today, let me spread kind words in honor of Your Son. Today, let forgiveness rule my heart. And every day, Lord, let my love for Christ be demonstrated through the acts of kindness that I offer to those who need the healing touch of the Master's hand.

Amen

A Little Silence

Be silent before the Lord and wait expectantly for Him.
PSALM 37:7 HOLMAN CSB

Do you ever wonder if God is really "right here, right now"? Do you wonder if God hears your prayers, if He understands your feelings, or if He really knows your heart? If so, you're not alone: lots of very faithful Christians have experienced periods of doubt. In fact, some of the biggest heroes in the Bible had plenty of doubts—and so, perhaps, will you. But when you have doubts, remember this: God isn't on a coffee break, and He hasn't moved out of town. God isn't taking a long vacation, and He isn't snoozing on the couch. He's right here, right now, listening to your thoughts and prayers, watching over your every move.

The Bible teaches that a wonderful way to get to know God is simply to be still and listen to Him. But sometimes, you may find it hard to slow down and listen. As the demands of everyday life weigh down upon you, you may be tempted to ignore God's presence or—worse yet—to rebel against His commandments. But, when you quiet yourself and acknowledge His presence, God touches your heart and restores your spirits. So why not let Him do it right now? If you really want to know Him better, silence is a wonderful place to start.

Growth takes place in quietness, in hidden ways,
in silence and solitude.
The process is not accessible to observation.

EUGENE PETERSON

If the pace and the push, the noise and the crowds are
getting to you, it's time to stop the nonsense and find
a place of solace to refresh your spirit.

CHARLES SWINDOLL

Silence is as fit a garment for devotion as
any other language.

C. H. SPURGEON

*Truly my soul silently waits for God;
from Him comes my salvation.*

PSALM 62:1 NKJV

I am not alone, because the Father is with Me.

JOHN 16:32 HOLMAN CSB

Draw near to God,
and He will draw near to you.

—

JAMES 4:8 HCSB

Today's Prayer

Dear Lord, in the quiet moments of this day,
I will turn my thoughts and prayers to You.
In silence I will sense Your presence, and I will
seek Your will for my life, knowing that when
I accept Your peace, I will be blessed today
and throughout eternity.

Amen

Tackling Tough Times

*God is our refuge and strength, always ready to help
in times of trouble. So we will not fear, even if earthquakes
come and mountains crumble to the sea.*

PSALM 46:1-2 NLT

From time to time, all of us have to face troubles and disappointments. When we do, God stands ready to protect us. Psalm 147 promises, "He heals the brokenhearted and bandages their wounds" (v. 3, NCV), but it doesn't say that He heals them instantly. Usually, it takes time for God to heal His children.

If you find yourself in any kind of trouble, pray about it and ask God for help. And then be patient. God will work things out, just as He has promised, but He will do it in His own time and according to His own plan.

Jesus does not say, "There is no storm."
He says, I am here, do not toss, but trust."

VANCE HAVNER

Your greatest ministry will likely come out
of your greatest hurt.

RICK WARREN

God will not permit any troubles to come upon us unless
He has a specific plan by which great blessing can
come out of the difficulty.

PETER MARSHALL

*I called to the Lord in my distress; I called to my God.
From His temple He heard my voice.*

2 SAMUEL 22:7 HOLMAN CSB

*I will be with you when you pass through the waters . . .
when you walk through the fire . . .
the flame will not burn you. For I the Lord your God,
the Holy One of Israel, and your Savior.*

ISAIAH 43:2-3 HOLMAN CSB

We are pressured in every way
but not crushed;
we are perplexed but not in despair.

—

2 Corinthians 4:8 HCSB

Today's Prayer

Lord, sometimes life is so difficult that
I can't see any hope for the future.
But with You, there is always hope. Keep me
mindful that there is nothing that
will happen today that
You and I can't handle together.
Amen

Devo 11

The Right Crowd

Love from the center of who you are; don't fake it. Run for dear life from evil; hold on for dear life to good. Be good friends who love deeply; practice playing second fiddle.
ROMANS 12:9-10 MSG

Are you hanging out with people who make you a better Christian, or are you spending time with people who encourage you to stray from your faith? The answer to this question will have a surprising impact on the condition of your spiritual health. Why? Because peer pressure is very real and very powerful. That's why one of the best ways to ensure that you follow Christ is to find fellow believers who are willing to follow Him with you.

Our world is filled with pressures: some good, some bad. The pressures that we feel to follow God's will and obey His commandments are positive pressures. God places them on our hearts so that we might act in accordance with His will. But we also face different pressures, ones that are definitely not from God. When we feel pressured to do things—or even to think thoughts—that lead us away from Him, we must beware. If we are to please God, we must resist the pressures that society seeks to impose upon us, and we must conform ourselves, instead, to His will, to His path, and to His Son.

A friend who loves will be more concerned about what is best for you than being accepted by you.

CHARLES STANLEY

Yes, the Spirit was sent to be our Counselor. Yes, Jesus speaks to us personally. But often he works through another human being.

JOHN ELDREDGE

A friend is one who makes me do my best.

OSWALD CHAMBERS

Friend, don't go along with evil. Model the good. The person who does good does God's work. The person who does evil falsifies God, doesn't know the first thing about God.

3 JOHN 1:11 MSG

My son, if sinners entice you, don't be persuaded.

PROVERBS 1:10 HOLMAN CSB

Do not be misled:

"Bad company corrupts good character."

1 CORINTHIANS 15:33 NIV

Today's Prayer

Thank You Lord, for my friends,
the people who enrich my life.
I pray for them today,
and ask Your blessings upon them . . .
and upon me.
Amen

Devo 12

Every Day with God

Morning by morning he wakens me and opens my understanding to his will. The Sovereign Lord has spoken to me, and I have listened.

ISAIAH 50:4-5 NLT

Want to know God better? Then schedule a meeting with Him every day. Daily life is a tapestry of habits, and no habit is more important to your spiritual health than the discipline of daily prayer and devotion to the Creator. When you begin each day with your head bowed and your heart lifted, you are reminded of God's love and God's laws.

Each day has 1,440 minutes—do you value your relationship with God enough to spend a few of those minutes with Him? He deserves that much of your time and more. But if you find that you're simply "too busy" for a daily chat with your Father in heaven, it's time to take a long, hard look at your priorities and your values.

If you've acquired the unfortunate habit of trying to "squeeze" God into the corners of your life, it's time to reshuffle the items on your to-do list by placing God first. God wants your undivided attention, not the leftovers of your day. So, if you haven't already done so, form the habit of spending quality time with your Creator. He deserves it . . . and so, for that matter, do you.

I suggest you discipline yourself to spend time daily in
a systematic reading of God's Word.
Make this "quiet time" a priority that nobody can change.

WARREN WIERSBE

We must appropriate the tender mercy of God every day
after conversion or problems quickly develop. We need his
grace daily in order to live a righteous life.

JIM CYMBALA

Wasted time of which we are later ashamed,
temptations we yield to, weaknesses, lethargy in our work,
disorder and lack of discipline in our thoughts and in
our interaction with others—all these frequently have
their root in neglecting prayer in the morning.

DIETRICH BONHOEFFER

*Truly my soul silently waits for God;
from Him comes my salvation.*

PSALM 62:1 NKJV

*May the words of my mouth and the thoughts of my heart
be pleasing to you, O Lord, my rock and my redeemer.*

PSALM 19:14 NLT

Stay clear of silly stories that
get dressed up as religion.
Exercise daily in God—
no spiritual flabbiness, please!

—

1 TIMOTHY 4:7 MSG

Today's Prayer

Lord, help me to hear Your direction
for my life in the quiet moments when I study
Your Holy Word. And as I go about my daily
activities, let everything that I say
and do be pleasing to You.

Amen

Devo 13

Too Much Stuff?

Don't collect for yourselves treasures on earth, where moth and rust destroy and where thieves break in and steal. But collect for yourselves treasures in heaven, where neither moth nor rust destroys, and where thieves don't break in and steal. For where your treasure is, there your heart will be also.

MATTHEW 6:19-21 HOLMAN CSB

Are you a guy who's overly concerned with the stuff that money can buy? Hopefully not. On the grand stage of a well-lived life, material possessions should play a rather small role. Of course, we all need the basic necessities of life, but once we meet those needs for ourselves and for our families, the piling up of possessions creates more problems than it solves. Our real riches, of course, are not of this world. We are never really rich until we are rich in spirit.

Our society is in love with money and the things that money can buy. God is not. God cares about people, not possessions, and so must we. We must, to the best of our abilities, love our neighbors as ourselves, and we must, to the best of our abilities, resist the mighty temptation to place possessions ahead of people.

Money, in and of itself, is not evil; worshipping money is. So today, as you prioritize matters of importance in your life, remember that God is almighty, but the dollar is not.

If you want to be truly happy, you won't find it on
an endless quest for more stuff. You'll find it in receiving
God's generosity and in passing that generosity along.

BILL HYBELS

When possessions become our god, we become
materialistic and greedy . . . and we forfeit
our contentment and our joy.

CHARLES SWINDOLL

He is no fool who gives what he cannot keep to gain
what he cannot lose.

JIM ELLIOT

*He who trusts in his riches will fall,
but the righteous will flourish . . . .*

PROVERBS 11:28 NKJV

*A man's life does not consist in the abundance
of his possessions.*

LUKE 12:15 NIV

Today's Prayer

Lord, my greatest possession is my relationship
with You through Jesus Christ. You have
promised that, when I first seek
Your kingdom and Your righteousness,
You will give me whatever I need. Let me trust
You completely, Lord, for my needs, both
material and spiritual, this day and always.

Amen

Devo 14

Who Will You Follow?

"Follow Me," Jesus told them, "and I will make you into fishers of men!" Immediately they left their nets and followed Him.

MARK 1:17-18 HOLMAN CSB

God's love for you is deeper and more profound than you can imagine. God's love for you is so great that He sent His only Son to this earth to die for your sins and to offer you the priceless gift of eternal life. Now, you must decide whether or not to accept God's gift. Will you ignore it or embrace it? Will you return it or neglect it? Will you accept Christ's love and build a lifelong relationship with Him, or will you turn away from Him and take a different path?

Your decision to allow Christ to reign over your heart is the pivotal decision of your life. It is a decision that you cannot ignore. It is a decision that is yours and yours alone. Accept God's gift now: allow His Son to preside over your heart, your thoughts, and your life, starting this very instant.

Christ is like a river that is continually flowing.
There are always fresh supplies of water coming from
the fountain-head, so that a man may live by it and be
supplied with water all his life. So Christ is an ever-flowing
fountain; he is continually supplying his people, and
the fountain is not spent. They who live upon Christ may
have fresh supplies from him for all eternity; they may have
an increase of blessedness that is new, and new still,
and which never will come to an end.

JONATHAN EDWARDS

Imagine the spiritual strength the disciples drew from
walking hundreds of miles with Jesus…3 John 4

JOHN MAXWELL

*Then he told them what they could expect for themselves:
"Anyone who intends to come with me has to let me lead."*
LUKE 9:23 MSG

*I've laid down a pattern for you.
What I've done, you do.*
JOHN 13:15 MSG

Today's Prayer

Dear Lord, You sent Jesus to save the world
and to save me. I thank You for Jesus,
and I will do my best to follow Him,
today and forever.
Amen

Devo 15

Time for a Celebration!

David and the whole house of Israel were celebrating with all their might before the LORD, with songs and with harps, lyres, tambourines, sistrums and cymbals.

2 SAMUEL 6:5 NIV

D o you feel like celebrating? If you're a believer, you should! When you allow Christ to reign over your heart, today and every day should be a time for joyful celebration.

What do you expect from the day ahead? Are you expecting God to do wonderful things, or are you living beneath a cloud of worry and doubt? The words of Psalm 118:24 remind us that every day is a gift from God. So whatever this day holds for you, begin it and end it with God as your partner and Christ as your Savior. And throughout the day, give thanks to the One who created you and saved you. God's love for you is infinite. Accept it; celebrate it; and be thankful.

Joy is the great note all throughout the Bible.

OSWALD CHAMBERS

Let God have you, and let God love you—and don't be surprised if your heart begins to hear music you've never heard and your feet learn to dance as never before.

MAX LUCADO

Some of us seem so anxious about avoiding hell that we forget to celebrate our journey toward heaven.

PHILIP YANCEY

Shout for joy to the LORD, all the earth.
Worship the LORD with gladness;
come before him with joyful songs.

PSALM 100:1-2 NIV

So now we can rejoice in our wonderful new relationship
with God—all because of what our Lord Jesus Christ
has done for us in making us friends of God.

ROMANS 5:11 NLT

This is the day the LORD has made;
we will rejoice and be glad in it.

PSALM 118:24 NKJV

Today's Prayer

Dear Lord, You have given me so many reasons to celebrate. Today, let me choose an attitude of cheerfulness. Let me be a joyful Christian, Lord, quick to laugh and slow to anger. Let me praise You, Lord, and give thanks for Your blessings. Today is Your creation; let me celebrate it . . . and You.

Amen

Devo 16

Radical Optimism

I can do everything through him that gives me strength.
PHILIPPIANS 4:13 NIV

Are you a radically optimistic believer? Do you believe that God has a wonderful plan that is perfectly suited for your life? And do you believe that when your life here on earth is done, you will enjoy the priceless gift of eternal life? Hopefully so, because Christianity and pessimism don't mix. Why? Because Christians have every reason to be optimistic about life here on earth and life eternal.

Sometimes, despite our trust in God, we may fall into the spiritual traps of worry, frustration, or sheer exhaustion, and our hearts become heavy. What's needed is plenty of rest, a large dose of perspective, and plenty of prayer, but not necessarily in that order.

Today, make this promise to yourself and keep it: vow to be a hope-filled Christian. Think optimistically about your life and your future. Trust your hopes, not your fears. Take time to celebrate God's glorious creation. And then, when you've filled your heart with hope and gladness, share your optimism with your friends. They'll be better for it, and so will you. But not necessarily in that order.

The popular idea of faith is of a certain obstinate optimism:
the hope, tenaciously held in the face of trouble,
that the universe is fundamentally friendly
and things may get better.

J. I. PACKER

It is a remarkable thing that some of the most optimistic
and enthusiastic people you will meet are those
who have been through intense suffering.

WARREN WIERSBE

*My cup runs over. Surely goodness and mercy
shall follow me all the days of my life;
and I will dwell in the house of the Lord Forever.*

PSALM 23:5-6 NKJV

*The Lord is my light and my salvation; whom shall I fear?
The Lord is the strength of my life;
of whom shall I be afraid?*

PSALM 27:1 KJV

Make me to hear joy and gladness....

PSALM 51:8 KJV

Be of good courage,
and he shall strengthen your heart,
all ye that hope in the LORD.

—

PSALM 31:24 KJV

Today's Prayer

Lord, You care for me, You love me, and You have given me the priceless gift of eternal life through Your Son Jesus. Because of You, Lord, I have every reason to live each day with celebration and hope. Help me to face this day with a spirit of optimism and thanksgiving so that I may lift the spirits of those I meet as I share the Good News of Your Son. And, let me focus my thoughts on You and Your incomparable gifts today and forever.

Amen

Too Impulsive?

He who guards his lips guards his life,
but he who speaks rashly will come to ruin.
Proverbs 13:3 NIV

Are you, at times, just a little bit impulsive? Do you occasionally leap before you look? Do you react first and think about your reaction second? If so, God wants to have a little chat with you.

God's Word is clear: as believers, we are called to lead lives of discipline, diligence, moderation, and maturity. But the world often tempts us to behave otherwise. Everywhere we turn, or so it seems, we are faced with powerful temptations to behave in undisciplined, ungodly ways.

God's Word instructs us to be disciplined in our thoughts and our actions; God's Word warns us against the dangers of impulsive behavior. God's Word teaches us that "anger" is only one letter away from "danger." And, as believers in a just God who means what He says, we should act—and react—accordingly.

Our challenge is to wait in faith for the day of
God's favor and salvation.

JIM CYMBALA

Grass that is here today and gone tomorrow does not
require much time to mature. A big oak tree that lasts for
generations requires much more time to grow and mature.
God is concerned about your life through eternity.
Allow Him to take all the time He needs to shape you
for His purposes. Larger assignments will require longer
periods of preparation.

HENRY BLACKABY

*The one who walks with the wise will become wise,
but a companion of fools will suffer harm.*

PROVERBS 13:20 HOLMAN CSB

*But if any of you needs wisdom, you should ask God for it.
He is generous and enjoys giving to all people,
so he will give you wisdom.*

JAMES 1:5 NCV

The wise inherit honor, but fools are put to shame!

PROVERBS 3:35 NLT

Those who are wise will shine
as bright as the sky,
and those who turn many to
righteousness will shine
like stars forever.

Daniel 12:3 NLT

Today's Prayer

Lord, sometimes I can be an impulsive person.
Slow me down, calm me down,
and help me make wise decisions . . .
today and every day of my life.
Amen

Devo 18

Extreme Faith

Whoever serves me must follow me.
Then my servant will be with me everywhere I am.
My Father will honor anyone who serves me.
JOHN 12:26 NCV

Jesus made an extreme sacrifice for you. Are you willing to make extreme changes in your life for Him? Can you honestly say that you're passionate about your faith and that you're really following Jesus? Hopefully so. But if you're preoccupied with other things—or if you're strictly a one-day-a-week Christian—then you're in need of an extreme spiritual makeover!

Jesus doesn't want you to be a run-of-the-mill, follow-the-crowd kind of guy. Jesus wants you to be a "new creation" through Him. And that's exactly what you should want for yourself, too. Nothing is more important than your wholehearted commitment to your Creator and to His only begotten Son. Your faith must never be an afterthought; it must be your ultimate priority, your ultimate possession, and your ultimate passion.

You are the recipient of Christ's love. Accept it enthusiastically and share it passionately. Jesus deserves your extreme enthusiasm; the world deserves it; and you deserve the experience of sharing it.

The essence of the Christian life is Jesus:
that in all things He might have the preeminence,
not that in some things He might have a place.

FRANKLIN GRAHAM

A disciple is a follower of Christ. That means you take on
His priorities as your own. His agenda becomes
your agenda. His mission becomes your mission.

CHARLES STANLEY

The heaviest end of the cross lies ever on His shoulders.
If He bids us carry a burden, He carries it also.

C. H. SPURGEON

*If you do not stand firm in your faith,
then you will not stand at all.*

ISAIAH 7:9 HOLMAN CSB

Be alert, stand firm in the faith, be brave and strong.

1 CORINTHIANS 16:13 HOLMAN CSB

Anything is possible if a person believes.

MARK 9:23 NLT

Today's Prayer

Dear Jesus, because I am Your disciple,
I will trust You, I will obey Your teachings,
and I will share Your Good News. You have
given me life abundant and life eternal,
and I will follow You today and forever.
Amen

Devo 19

Real Joy

I've told you these things for a purpose:
that my joy might be your joy, and your joy wholly mature.
JOHN 15:11 MSG

Christ made it clear: He intends that His joy should become our joy. Yet sometimes, amid the inevitable hustle and bustle of life-here-on-earth, we can forfeit—albeit temporarily—the joy of Christ as we wrestle with the challenges of daily living.

Billy Graham correctly observed, "When Jesus Christ is the source of our joy, no words can describe it." And C. S. Lewis noted that, "Joy is the serious business of heaven."

You can't really get to know God until you genuinely experience God's joy for yourself. It's not enough to hear somebody else talk about being a joyful Christian—you must experience Christ's joy in order to understand it. Does that mean that you'll be a joy-filled believer 24 hours a day, seven days a week, from this moment on? Nope. But it does mean that you can experience God's joy personally, frequently, intensely.

So here's a prescription for better spiritual health: Open the door of your soul to Christ. When you do, He will give you peace and joy . . . heaping helpings of peace and joy.

I choose joy. I will refuse the temptation to be cynical;
cynicism is the tool of a lazy thinker. I will refuse to see
people as anything less than human beings, created by God.
I will refuse to see any problem as anything less than
an opportunity to see God.

MAX LUCADO

Joy comes from knowing God loves me and knows
who I am and where I'm going . . .
that my future is secure as I rest in Him.

JAMES DOBSON

When I met Christ, I felt that I had swallowed sunshine.

E. STANLEY JONES

Rejoice in the Lord always. I will say it again: Rejoice!

PHILIPPIANS 4:4 HOLMAN CSB

*Delight yourself also in the Lord,
and He shall give you the desires of your heart.*

PSALM 37:4 NKJV

Today's Prayer

Dear Lord, You have given me so many blessings; let me celebrate Your gifts. Make me thankful, loving, responsible, and wise. I praise You, Father, for the gift of Your Son and for the priceless gift of salvation. Make me be a joyful Christian and a worthy example to my loved ones, today and every day.

Amen

Devo 20

The Marathon

For you need endurance, so that after you have done God's will, you may receive what was promised.

HEBREWS 10:36 HOLMAN CSB

Are you one of those guys who doesn't give up easily, or are you quick to bail out when the going gets tough? If you've developed the unfortunate habit of giving up at the first sign of trouble, it's probably time for you to have a heart-to-heart talk with the guy you see every time you look in the mirror.

A well-lived life is like a marathon, not a sprint—it calls for preparation, determination, and lots of perseverance. As an example of perfect perseverance, you need look no further than your Savior, Jesus Christ.

Jesus finished what He began. Despite His suffering, despite the shame of the cross, Jesus was steadfast in His faithfulness to God. You, too, should remain faithful, especially when times are tough.

Are you facing a difficult situation? If so, remember this: whatever your problem, God can handle it. Your job is to keep persevering until He does.

Battles are won in the trenches, in the grit and grime of courageous determination; they are won day by day in the arena of life.

CHARLES SWINDOLL

Jesus taught that perseverance is the essential element in prayer.

E. M. BOUNDS

Perseverance is more than endurance. It is endurance combined with absolute assurance and certainty that what we are looking for is going to happen.

OSWALD CHAMBERS

*Let us not become weary in doing good,
for at the proper time we will reap a harvest
if we do not give up.*

GALATIANS 6:9 NIV

*But as for you, be strong; don't be discouraged,
for your work has a reward.*

2 CHRONICLES 15:7 HOLMAN CSB

Today's Prayer

Lord, when life is difficult, I am tempted to abandon hope in the future. But You are my God, and I can draw strength from You. Let me trust You, Father, in good times and in bad times. Let me persevere—even if my soul is troubled—and let me follow Your Son Jesus Christ this day and forever.

Amen

Devo 21

Beyond Anger

But now you must also put away all the following:
anger, wrath, malice, slander,
and filthy language from your mouth.
COLOSSIANS 3:8 HOLMAN CSB

The frustrations of everyday living can sometimes get the better of us, and we allow minor disappointments to cause us major problems. When we allow ourselves to become overly irritated by the inevitable ups and downs of life, we become overstressed, overheated, overanxious, and just plain angry.

When you allow yourself to become angry, you are certain to defeat at least one person: yourself. When you allow the minor frustrations of everyday life to hijack your emotions, you do harm to yourself and to your loved ones. So today and every day, guard yourself against the kind of angry thinking that inevitably takes a toll on your emotions and your relationships.

As the old saying goes, "Anger usually improves nothing but the arch of a cat's back." So don't allow feelings of anger or frustration to rule your life, or, for that matter, your day—your life is simply too short for that, and you deserve much better treatment than that . . . from yourself.

When you strike out in anger, you may miss the other person, but you will always hit yourself.

JIM GALLERY

Anger is the noise of the soul; the unseen irritant of the heart; the relentless invader of silence.

MAX LUCADO

Is there somebody who's always getting your goat? Talk to the Shepherd.

ANONYMOUS

Don't become angry quickly,
because getting angry is foolish.
ECCLESIASTES 7:9 NCV

When you are angry, do not sin,
and be sure to stop being angry before the end of the day.
Do not give the devil a way to defeat you.
EPHESIANS 4:26–27 NCV

My dearly loved brothers,
understand this:
everyone must be quick to hear,
slow to speak, and slow to anger,
for man's anger does not accomplish
God's righteousness.

—

James 1:19-20 HCSB

Today's Prayer

Lord, sometimes, I am quick to anger and slow to forgive. But I know, Lord, that You seek abundance and peace for my life. Forgiveness is Your commandment; empower me to follow the example of Your Son Jesus who forgave His persecutors. As I turn away from anger, I claim the peace that You intend for my life.

Amen

Devo 22

Too Busy to Pray?

If my people who are called by my name, will humble themselves and pray and seek my face and turn from their wicked ways, then will I hear from heaven and will forgive their sin and will heal their land.

2 Chronicles 7:14 NIV

Is prayer an integral part of your daily life, or is it a hit-or-miss habit? Do you "pray without ceasing," or is your prayer life an afterthought? Do you regularly pray in the quiet moments of the early morning, or do you bow your head only when others are watching? If your prayers have become more a matter of habit than a matter of passion, you're robbing yourself of a deeper relationship with God. And how can you rectify this situation? By praying more frequently and more fervently.

The quality of your spiritual life will be in direct proportion to the quality of your prayer life: the more you pray, the closer you will feel to God. So today, instead of turning things over in your mind, turn them over to God in prayer. Don't limit your prayers to the dinner table or the bedside table. Pray constantly about things great and small. God is always listening . . . and the rest is up to you.

God shapes the world by prayer. The more praying there is
in the world, the better the world will be,
and the mightier will be the forces against evil.

E. M. BOUNDS

Prayer connects us with God's limitless potential.

HENRY BLACKABY

God wants to remind us that nothing on earth or in hell
can ultimately stand against the man or the woman
who calls on the name of the Lord!

JIM CYMBALA

*The effective prayer of a righteous man
can accomplish much.*

JAMES 5:16 NASB

*Whatever you ask for in prayer,
believe that you have received it, and it will be yours.*

MARK 11:24 NIV

Rejoice evermore.
Pray without ceasing.
In every thing give thanks:
for this is the will of God in Christ Jesus
concerning you.

—

1 Thessalonians 5:16-18 KJV

Today's Prayer

Dear Lord, I will open my heart to You.
I will take my concerns, my fears, my plans,
and my hopes to You in prayer. And, then,
I will trust the answers that You give. You are
my loving Father, and I will accept Your will
for my life today and every day that I live.
Amen

Devo 23

God Can Handle It

Cast your burden on the Lord, and He will support you;
He will never allow the righteous to be shaken.

PSALM 55:22 HOLMAN CSB

It's a promise that is made over and over again in the Bible: Whatever "it" is, God can handle it. Life isn't always easy. Far from it! Sometimes, life can be very, very tough. But even then, even during our darkest moments, we're protected by a loving Heavenly Father. When we're worried, God can reassure us; when we're sad, God can comfort us. When our hearts are broken, God is not just near, He is here. So we must lift our thoughts and prayers to Him. When we do, He will answer our prayers. Why? Because He is our shepherd, and He has promised to protect us now and forever.

You may not know what you are going to do;
you only know that God knows what He is going to do.

OSWALD CHAMBERS

The next time you're disappointed, don't panic.
Don't give up. Just be patient and
let God remind you he's still in control.

MAX LUCADO

We do not understand the intricate pattern of the stars in
their course, but we know that He who created them does,
and that just as surely as He guides them,
He is charting a safe course for us.

BILLY GRAHAM

God—His way is perfect; the word of the Lord is pure.
He is a shield to all who take refuge in Him.

PSALM 18:30 HOLMAN CSB

The Lord is my rock, my fortress, and my deliverer.

PSALM 18:2 HOLMAN CSB

Today's Prayer

Dear Lord, You rule over our world, and I will allow You to rule over my heart. I will obey Your commandments, I will study Your Word, and I will seek Your will for my life, today and every day of my life.
Amen

Who Rules?

First pay attention to me, and then relax.
Now you can take it easy—you're in good hands.
PROVERBS 1:33 MSG

Is God a big priority for you . . . or is He an afterthought?
Do you give God your best or what's left? Have you given
Christ your heart, your soul, your talents, your time, and
your testimony? Or are you giving Him little more than a few
hours each Sunday morning?

In the book of Exodus, God warns that we should
place no gods before Him (Exodus 20:3). Yet all too often,
we place our Lord in second, third, or fourth place as we
worship the gods of pride, money, or personal gratification.
When we unwittingly place possessions or relationships
above our love for the Creator, we must realign our priorities
or suffer the consequences.

Does God rule your heart? Make certain that the honest
answer to this question is a resounding yes. In the life of
every radical believer, God comes first. And that's precisely
the place that He deserves in your heart.

No test of a man's true character is more conclusive
than how he spends his time and his money.

PATRICK MORLEY

Having values keeps a person focused on
the important things.

JOHN MAXWELL

He is no fool who gives what he cannot keep
to gain what he cannot lose.

JIM ELLIOT

*And I pray this: that your love will keep on growing in
knowledge and every kind of discernment, so that you
can determine what really matters and can be pure and
blameless in the day of Christ.*

PHILIPPIANS 1:9 HOLMAN CSB

*So teach us to number our days,
that we may gain a heart of wisdom.*

PSALM 90:12 NKJV

Today's Prayer

Dear Lord, today is a new day. Help me finish the important tasks first, even if those tasks are unpleasant. Don't let me put off until tomorrow what I should do today.

Amen

Devo 25

When Mountains Need Moving

*I assure you: If anyone says to this mountain,
"Be lifted up and thrown into the sea," and does not doubt in
his heart, but believes that what he says will happen,
it will be done for him.*

MARK 11:23 HOLMAN CSB

Because we live in a demanding world, all of us have mountains to climb and mountains to move. Moving those mountains requires faith.

Are you a mountain-moving guy whose faith is evident for all to see? Or, are you a spiritual underachiever? As you think about the answer to that question, consider this: God needs more people who are willing to move mountains for His glory and for His kingdom.

When you place your faith, your trust, indeed your life in the hands of your Heavenly Father, you'll be amazed at the marvelous things He can do with you and through you. So strengthen your faith through praise, through worship, through Bible study, and through prayer. And trust God's plans. With Him, all things are possible, and He stands ready to open a world of possibilities to you . . . if you have faith. And now, with no more delays, let the mountain moving begin.

Only God can move mountains,
but faith and prayer can move God.

E. M. BOUNDS

Faith is confidence in the promises of God or confidence
that God will do what He has promised.

CHARLES STANLEY

I do not want merely to possess a faith;
I want a faith that possesses me.

CHARLES KINGSLEY

*Now without faith it is impossible to please God,
for the one who draws near to Him must believe that
He exists and rewards those who seek Him.*

HEBREWS 11:6 HOLMAN CSB

*If you do not stand firm in your faith,
then you will not stand at all.*

ISAIAH 7:9 HOLMAN CSB

FOR GUYS

For we walk by faith, not by sight.

2 CORINTHIANS 5:7 HCSB

Today's Prayer

Dear Lord, I want faith that moves mountains.
You have big plans for this world and big plans
for me. Help me fulfill those plans, Father,
as I follow in the footsteps of Your Son.
Amen

Devo 26

The Search for Purpose

For everything, absolutely everything, above and below,
visible and invisible, rank after rank after rank of
angels—everything got started in him
and finds its purpose in him.

COLOSSIANS 1:16 MSG

"What on earth does God intend for me to do with my life?" It's an easy question to ask but, for many of us, a difficult question to answer. Why? Because God's purposes aren't always clear to us. Sometimes we wander aimlessly in a wilderness of our own making. And sometimes, we struggle mightily against God in an unsuccessful attempt to find success and happiness through our own means, not His.

Are you genuinely trying to figure out God's purpose for your life? If so, you can be sure that with God's help, you will eventually discover it. So keep praying, and keep watching. And rest assured: God's got big plans for you . . . very big plans.

Oh Lord, let me not live to be useless.

JOHN WESLEY

We must focus on prayer as the main thrust to accomplish
God's will and purpose on earth. The forces against us have
never been greater, and this is the only way we can
release God's power to become victorious.

JOHN MAXWELL

When God speaks to you through the Bible, prayer,
circumstances, the church, or in some other way,
he has a purpose in mind for your life.

HENRY BLACKABY AND CLAUDE KING

Whatever you do, do all to the glory of God.
1 CORINTHIANS 10:31 NKJV

I will instruct you and show you the way to go;
with My eye on you, I will give counsel.
PSALM 32:8 HOLMAN CSB

Commit your activities to the Lord
and your plans will be achieved.

—

PROVERBS 16:3 HCSB

Today's Prayer

Dear Lord, let Your purposes be my purposes.
Let Your priorities be my priorities.
Let Your will be my will. Let Your Word
be my guide. And, let me grow in faith
and in wisdom today and every day.

Amen

Devo 27

Need Strength?

Create in me a pure heart, O God, and renew a steadfast spirit within me. Do not cast me from your presence or take your Holy Spirit from me. Restore to me the joy of your salvation and grant me a willing spirit, to sustain me.

PSALM 51:10-12 NIV

Even the most inspired Christian guys can find themselves running on empty. Even the most well-intentioned guys can run out of energy; even the most hopeful believers can be burdened by fears and doubts. And you are no exception.

When you're exhausted or worried—or worse—there is a source from which you can draw the power needed to recharge your spiritual batteries. That source is God.

Are you tired or troubled? Turn your heart toward God in prayer. Are you weak or worried? Take the time—or, more accurately, make the time—to delve deeply into God's Holy Word. Are you spiritually depleted? Call upon fellow believers to support you, and call upon Christ to renew your spirit and your life. When you do, you'll discover that the Creator of the universe stands always ready and always able to create a new sense of wonderment and joy in you.

The resurrection of Jesus Christ is the power of God to change history and to change lives.

BILL BRIGHT

Walking with God leads to receiving his intimate counsel, and counseling leads to deep restoration.

JOHN ELDREDGE

One reason so much American Christianity is a mile wide and an inch deep is that Christians are simply tired. Sometimes you need to kick back and rest for Jesus' sake.

DENNIS SWANBERG

He said unto me, My grace is sufficient for thee: for my strength is made perfect in weakness.

2 CORINTHIANS 12:9 KJV

Whatever your hand finds to do, do it with all your might . . . .

ECCLESIASTES 9:10 NIV

Those who hope in the LORD
will renew their strength.
They will soar on wings like eagles;
they will run and not grow weary,
they will walk and not be faint.

—

ISAIAH 40:31 NIV

Today's Prayer

Dear Lord, sometimes the demands of the day leave me discouraged and frustrated. Renew my strength, Father, and give me patience and perspective. Today and every day, let me draw comfort and courage from Your promises, from Your love, and from Your Son.

Amen

Devo 28

Discipline Now

But I discipline my body and bring it into subjection,
lest, when I have preached to others,
I myself should become disqualified.
1 CORINTHIANS 9:27 NKJV

Are you a self-disciplined guy? If so, congratulations . . .
if not, God wants to have a little talk with you. God
doesn't reward laziness, misbehavior, or apathy. To
the contrary, He expects His followers to behave with dignity
and discipline. But sometimes, it's extremely difficult to be
dignified and disciplined. Why? Because the world wants us
to believe that dignified, self-disciplined behavior is going
out of style.

You live in a world in which leisure is glorified and
indifference is often glamorized. But God has other plans.
He did not create you to be ordinary; He created you for far
greater things.

Face facts: Life's greatest rewards aren't likely to fall into
your lap. To the contrary, your greatest accomplishments
will probably require lots of work, which is perfectly fine with
God. After all, He knows that you're up to the task, and He
has big plans for you. God will do His part to fulfill those
plans, and the rest, of course, is up to you.

The alternative to discipline is disaster.

VANCE HAVNER

If one examines the secret behind a championship
football team, a magnificent orchestra, or a successful
business, the principal ingredient is invariably discipline.

JAMES DOBSON

Personal humility is a spiritual discipline
and the hallmark of the service of Jesus.

FRANKLIN GRAHAM

Discipline yourself for the purpose of godliness.

1 TIMOTHY 4:7 NASB

*Do you not know that those who run in a race all run,
but only one receives the prize? Run in such a way
that you may win. Everyone who competes in the games
exercises self-control in all things.*

1 CORINTHIANS 9:24-25 NASB

God hasn't invited us into
a disorderly, unkempt life but into
something holy and beautiful—
as beautiful on the inside as the outside.

—

1 THESSALONIANS 4:7 MSG

Today's Prayer

Heavenly Father, make me a young man of
discipline and righteousness.
Let me teach others
by the faithfulness of my conduct,
and let me follow Your will and Your Word,
today and every day.
Amen

Devo 29

Good Decision

God's Way is not a matter of mere talk;
it's an empowered life.
1 CORINTHIANS 4:20 MSG

Everyday life is an adventure in decision-making. Each day, we make countless decisions that hopefully bring us closer to God. When we obey God's commandments, we share in His abundance and His peace. But, when we turn our backs upon God by disobeying Him, we invite Old Man Trouble to stop by for an extended visit.

Do you want to be successful and happy? If so, here's a good place to start: Obey God. When you're faced with a difficult choice or a powerful temptation, pray about it. Invite God into your heart and live according to His commandments. When you do, you will be blessed today, tomorrow, and forever.

It may be said without qualification that every man is
as holy and as full of the Spirit as he wants to be.
He may not be as full as he wishes he were,
but he is most certainly as full as he wants to be.

A. W. TOZER

Righteousness not only defines God,
but God defines righteousness.

BILL HYBELS

If we don't hunger and thirst after righteousness,
we'll become anemic and feel miserable in
our Christian experience.

FRANKLIN GRAHAM

Now if any of you lacks wisdom, he should ask God,
who gives to all generously and without criticizing,
and it will be given to him. But let him ask in faith
without doubting. For the doubter is like the surging sea,
driven and tossed by the wind.

JAMES 1:5-6 HOLMAN CSB

Even zeal is not good without knowledge,
and the one who acts hastily sins.

—

PROVERBS 19:2 HCSB

Today's Prayer

Lord, it is so much easier to speak of
the righteous life than it is to live it. Let me live
righteously, and let my actions be consistent
with my beliefs. Let every step that I take reflect
Your truth, and let me live a life
that is worthy of Your Son.
Amen

Devo 30

Gimme Patience!

Be gentle to everyone, able to teach, and patient.
2 TIMOTHY 2:23 HOLMAN CSB

Are you a perfectly patient fellow? If so, feel free to skip the rest of this page. But if you're not, here's something to think about: If you really want to become a more patient person, God is ready and willing to help.

The Bible promises that when you sincerely seek God's help, He will give you the things that you need—and that includes patience. But God won't force you to become a more patient person. If you want to become a more mature Christian, you've got to do some of the work yourself—and the best time to start doing that work is now.

So, if you want to gain patience and maturity, bow your head and start praying about it. Then, rest assured that with God's help, you can most certainly make yourself a more patient, understanding, mature Christian.

As we wait on God, He helps us use the winds of adversity to soar above our problems. As the Bible says, "Those who wait on the LORD…shall mount up with wings like eagles."

BILLY GRAHAM

You can't step in front of God and not get in trouble. When He says, "Go three steps," don't go four.

CHARLES STANLEY

In all negotiations of difficulties, a man may not look to sow and reap at once. He must prepare his business and so ripen it by degrees.

FRANCIS BACON

Patience and encouragement come from God. And I pray that God will help you all agree with each other the way Christ Jesus wants.

ROMANS 15:5 NCV

But if we look forward to something we don't have yet, we must wait patiently and confidently.

ROMANS 8:25 NLT

God has chosen you and made you
his holy people. He loves you.
So always do these things:
Show mercy to others, be kind, humble,
gentle, and patient.

—

COLOSSIANS 3:12 NCV

Today's Prayer

Heavenly Father, let me wait quietly for You.
Let me live according to Your plan
and according to Your timetable.
When I am hurried, slow me down.
When I become impatient with others, give
me empathy. Today, I want to be a patient
Christian, Dear Lord, as I trust in You
and in Your master plan.
Amen

Devo 31

A Willingness to Serve

You address me as "Teacher" and "Master," and rightly so.
That is what I am. So if I, the Master and Teacher,
washed your feet, you must now wash each other's feet.
I've laid down a pattern for you. What I've done, you do.
JOHN 13:15 MSG

The words of Jesus are clear: the most esteemed men and women in this world are not the big-shots who jump up on stage and hog the spotlight; the greatest among us are those who are willing to become humble servants.

Are you willing to become a servant for Christ? Are you willing to pitch in and make the world a better place, or are you determined to keep all your blessings to yourself? Hopefully, you are determined to follow Christ's example by making yourself an unselfish servant to those who need your help.

Today, you may be tempted to take more than you give. But if you feel the urge to be selfish, resist that urge with all your might. Don't be stingy, selfish, or self-absorbed. Instead, serve your friends quietly and without fanfare. Find a need and fill it . . . humbly. Lend a helping hand . . . anonymously. Share a word of kindness . . . with quiet sincerity. As you go about your daily activities, remember that the Savior of all humanity made Himself a servant, and we, as His followers, must do no less.

Make it a rule, and pray to God to help you to keep it, never, if possible, to lie down at night without being able to say: "I have made one human being at least a little wiser, or a little happier, or at least a little better this day."

CHARLES KINGSLEY

In Jesus, the service of God and the service of the least of the brethren were one.

DIETRICH BONHOEFFER

God does not do anything with us, only through us.

OSWALD CHAMBERS

If they serve Him obediently, they will end their days in prosperity and their years in happiness.

JOB 36:11 HOLMAN CSB

A person should consider us in this way: as servants of Christ and managers of God's mysteries. In this regard, it is expected of managers that each one be found faithful.

1 CORINTHIANS 4:1-2 HOLMAN CSB

Worship the Lord your God and . . .
serve Him only.

—

MATTHEW 4:10 HCSB

Today's Prayer

Dear Lord, when Jesus humbled Himself
and became a servant, He also became
an example for me. Make me a faithful steward
of my gifts, and let me be a humble servant
to my loved ones, to my friends,
and to those in need.

Amen

Devo 32

Choices

*I am offering you life or death, blessings or curses.
Now, choose life! . . . To choose life is to love
the Lord your God, obey him, and stay close to him.*
DEUTERONOMY 30:19-20 NCV

Face facts: your life is a series of choices. From the instant you wake up in the morning until the moment you nod off to sleep at night, you make countless decisions—decisions about the things you do, decisions about the words you speak, and decisions about the way that you choose to direct your thoughts.

As a believer who has been transformed by the radical love of Jesus, you have every reason to make wise choices. But sometimes, when the daily grind threatens to grind you up and spit you out, you may make choices that are displeasing to God. When you do, you'll pay a price because you'll forfeit the happiness and the peace that might otherwise have been yours.

So, as you pause to consider the kind of Christian you are—and the kind of Christian you want to become—ask yourself whether you're sitting on the fence or standing in the light. And then, if you sincerely want to follow in the footsteps of the One from Galilee, make choices that are pleasing to Him. He deserves no less . . . and neither, for that matter, do you.

We are either the masters or the victims of our attitudes.
It is a matter of personal choice. Who we are today is
the result of choices we made yesterday. Tomorrow,
we will become what we choose today.
To change means to choose to change.

JOHN MAXWELL

Life is a series of choices between the bad, the good,
and the best. Everything depends on how we choose.

VANCE HAVNER

Every day, I find countless opportunities to decide
whether I will obey God and demonstrate my love for Him
or try to please myself or the world system.
God is waiting for my choices.

BILL BRIGHT

*The thing you should want most is God's kingdom
and doing what God wants.
Then all these other things you need will be given to you.*

MATTHEW 6:33 NCV

So I strive always to keep my conscience
clear before God and man.

ACTS 24:16 NIV

Today's Prayer

Heavenly Father, I have many choices to make.
Help me choose wisely as I follow
in the footsteps of Your only begotten Son.
Amen

Devo 33

Fully Grown?

*Therefore, leaving the elementary message about
the Messiah, let us go on to maturity.*
HEBREWS 6:1 HOLMAN CSB

Are you about as mature as you're ever going to be? Hopefully not! When it comes to your faith, God doesn't intend for you to become "fully grown," at least not in this lifetime.

As a Christian, you should continue to grow in the love and the knowledge of your Savior as long as you live. How? By studying God's Word, by obeying His commandments, and by allowing His Son to reign over your heart.

Are you continually seeking to become a more mature believer? Hopefully so, because that's exactly what you owe to God and to yourself.

I've never met anyone who became instantly mature. It's a painstaking process that God takes us through, and it includes such things as waiting, failing, losing, and being misunderstood—each calling for extra doses of perseverance.

CHARLES SWINDOLL

The Scriptures were not given for our information, but for our transformation.

D. L. MOODY

A person who gazes and keeps on gazing at Jesus becomes like him in appearance.

E. STANLEY JONES

For this reason we also, since the day we heard it, do not cease to pray for you, and to ask that you may be filled with the knowledge of His will in all wisdom and spiritual understanding

COLOSSIANS 1:9 NKJV

Run away from infantile indulgence. Run after mature righteousness—faith, love, peace—joining those who are in honest and serious prayer before God.

2 TIMOTHY 2:22 MSG

Today's Prayer

Dear Lord, the Bible tells me that You are at work in my life, continuing to help me grow and to mature in my faith. Show me Your wisdom, Father, and let me live according to Your Word and Your will.

Amen

Devo 34

Saying "Thanks" to God

Give thanks in all circumstances;
for this is God's will for you in Christ Jesus.
1 THESSALONIANS 5:18 NIV

Are you basically a thankful guy? Do you appreciate the stuff you've got and the life that you're privileged to live? You most certainly should be thankful. After all, when you stop to think about it, God has given you more blessings than you can count. So the question of the day is this: will you slow down long enough to thank your Heavenly Father . . . or not?

Sometimes, life-here-on-earth can be complicated, demanding, and frustrating. When the demands of life leave you rushing from place to place with scarcely a moment to spare, you may fail to pause and thank your Creator for the countless blessings He has given you. Failing to thank God is understandable . . . but it's wrong.

God's Word makes it clear: a wise heart is a thankful heart. Period. Your Heavenly Father has blessed you beyond measure, and you owe Him everything, including your thanks. God is always listening—are you willing to say thanks? It's up to you, and the next move is yours.

It is only with gratitude that life becomes rich.

DIETRICH BONHOEFFER

We ought to give thanks for all fortune: if it is good,
because it is good, if bad, because it works in us patience,
humility, and the contempt of this world along
with the hope of our eternal country.

C. S. LEWIS

The words "thank" and "think" come from the same
root word. If we would think more, we would thank more.

WARREN WIERSBE

Give thanks to the Lord, for He is good;
His faithful love endures forever.

PSALM 118:29 HOLMAN CSB

Our prayers for you are always spilling over into
thanksgivings. We can't quit thanking God our
Father and Jesus our Messiah for you!

COLOSSIANS 1:3 MSG

Today's Prayer

Dear Lord, today I will thank You
for all Your blessings. And I'll do the same
thing tomorrow, and every day after that.
You never stop loving me,
and I will never stop praising You.
Amen

Devo 35

Getting the Work Done

Do not be lazy but work hard,
serving the Lord with all your heart.
ROMANS 12:11 NCV

Have you acquired the habit of doing first things first, or are you one of those guys who puts off important work until the last minute? The answer to this simple question will help determine how well you do your work and how much fun you have doing it.

God's Word teaches us the value of hard work. In his second letter to the Thessalonians, Paul warns, " …if any would not work, neither should he eat" (3:10 KJV). And the Book of Proverbs proclaims, "One who is slack in his work is brother to one who destroys" (18:9 NIV). In short, God has created a world in which diligence is rewarded and laziness is not. So, whatever it is that you choose to do, do it with commitment, excitement, and vigor. And remember this: Hard work is not simply a proven way to get ahead, it's also part of God's plan for you.

You have countless opportunities to accomplish great things for God—but you should not expect the work to be easy. So pray as if everything depended upon God, but work as if everything depended upon you. When you do, you should expect very big payoffs because when you and God become partners in your work, amazing things happen.

If you want to reach your potential,
you need to add a strong work ethic to your talent.

JOHN MAXWELL

Chiefly the mold of a man's fortune is in his own hands.

FRANCIS BACON

People who work for money only are usually miserable,
because there is no fulfillment
and no meaning to what they do.

DAVE RAMSEY

*Whatever you do, do it enthusiastically,
as something done for the Lord and not for men.*

COLOSSIANS 3:23 HOLMAN CSB

Whatever your hands find to do, do with [all] your strength.

ECCLESIASTES 9:10 HOLMAN CSB

He did it with all his heart. So he prospered.

2 CHRONICLES 31:21 NKJV

Don't work only while being watched,
in order to please men, but as slaves
of Christ, do God's will from your heart.
Render service with a good attitude,
as to the Lord and not to men.

—

EPHESIANS 6:6-7 HCSB

Today's Prayer

Lord, let me be an industrious worker
in Your fields. Those fields are ripe, Lord, and
Your workers are few. Let me be counted as
Your faithful, diligent servant today,
and every day.
Amen

Devo 36

The Wisdom of Waiting

God wants you to live a pure life. Keep yourselves from sexual promiscuity. Learn to appreciate and give dignity to your body, not abusing it, as is so common among those who know nothing of God.

1 THESSALONIANS 4:3-5 MSG

You live in a society that is filled to the brim with temptations, distractions, and distortions about sex. You are bombarded with images that glamorize sex outside marriage. In fact, you are subjected to daily pressures and problems that were largely unknown to earlier generations. At every corner, or so it seems, you are confronted with the message that premarital sex is a harmless activity, something that should be considered "recreational." That message is a terrible lie with tragic consequences.

When you think about it, the argument in favor of abstinence isn't a very hard case to make. First and foremost, abstinence is a part of God's plan for people who are not married. Period. But it doesn't stop there: abstinence is also the right thing to do and the smart thing to do.

God has a plan for your life, a plan that does not include sex before marriage. So do yourself a favor: take time to think carefully about the wisdom of waiting. It's your choice. Please choose wisely.

To many, total abstinence is easier
than perfect moderation.

St. Augustine

Be patient. God is using today's difficulties to strengthen
you for tomorrow. He is equipping you.
The God who makes things grow will help you bear fruit.

Max Lucado

To wait upon God is the perfection of activity.

Oswald Chambers

Sow righteousness for yourselves and reap faithful love;
break up your untilled ground.
It is time to seek the Lord until He comes
and sends righteousness on you like the rain.

Hosea 10:12 Holman CSB

Blessed are the pure in heart, for they shall see God.

Matthew 5:8 NKJV

Do you not know that your body is
a sanctuary of the Holy Spirit who is
in you, whom you have from God?
You are not your own,
for you were bought at a price;
therefore glorify God in your body.

1 CORINTHIANS 6:19-20 HCSB

Today's Prayer

Dear Lord, Your Word makes it clear I am to honor You by honoring my body. In every decision that I make, I will obey my conscience and obey Your Holy Word.

Amen.

Devo 37

Courage for Difficult Days

Be strong and courageous, and do the work.
Do not be afraid or discouraged,
for the Lord God, my God, is with you.
1 CHRONICLES 28:20 NIV

Life-here-on-earth can be difficult and discouraging at times. During our darkest moments, God offers us strength and courage if we turn our hearts and our prayers to Him.

As believing Christians, we have every reason to live courageously. After all, the ultimate battle has already been fought and won on the cross at Calvary. But sometimes, because we are imperfect human beings who possess imperfect faith, we fall prey to fear and doubt. The answer to our fears, of course, is God.

The next time you find your courage tested to the limit, remember that God is as near as your next breath. He is your shield and your strength; He is your protector and your deliverer. Call upon Him in your hour of need and then be comforted. Whatever your challenge, whatever your trouble, God can handle it . . . and will!

The fear of God is the death of every other fear.

C. H. SPURGEON

Take courage. We walk in the wilderness today
and in the Promised Land tomorrow.

D. L. MOODY

Do not let Satan deceive you into being afraid
of God's plans for your life.

R. A. TORREY

*I called to the Lord in my distress; I called to my God.
From His temple He heard my voice.*

2 SAMUEL 22:7 HOLMAN CSB

*Consider it a great joy, my brothers, whenever you
experience various trials, knowing that the testing
of your faith produces endurance. But endurance must do its
complete work, so that you may be mature
and complete, lacking nothing.*

JAMES 1:2-4 HOLMAN CSB

Today's Prayer

Lord, sometimes, this world is a fearful place.
Yet, You have promised me that You are with
me always. With You as my protector,
I am not afraid. Today, Dear Lord, I will live
courageously as I place my trust in
Your everlasting power and my faith in
Your everlasting love.

Amen

Devo 38

Considering the Cross

*But as for me, I will never boast about anything except
the cross of our Lord Jesus Christ, through whom the world
has been crucified to me, and I to the world.*

GALATIANS 6:14 HOLMAN CSB

As we consider Christ's sacrifice on the cross, we
should be profoundly humbled and profoundly
grateful. And today, as we come to Christ in prayer,
we should do so in a spirit of quiet, heartfelt devotion to the
One who gave His life so that we might have life eternal.

He was the Son of God, but He wore a crown of thorns.
He was the Savior of mankind, yet He was put to death on
a roughhewn cross made of wood. He offered His healing
touch to an unsaved world, and yet the same hands that had
healed the sick and raised the dead were pierced with nails.

Christ humbled Himself on a cross—for you. He shed
His blood—for you. He has offered to walk with you through
this life and throughout all eternity. As you approach Him
today in prayer, think about His sacrifice and His grace. And
be humble.

Come and see the victories of the cross.
Christ's wounds are thy healings. His agonies, thy repose.
His death, thy life. His sufferings, thy salvation.

MATTHEW HENRY

No man understands the Scriptures unless he is
acquainted with the cross.

MARTIN LUTHER

There is no detour to holiness. Jesus came to
the resurrection through the cross, not around it.

LEIGHTON FORD

*For Christ also suffered once for sins, the just for the unjust,
that He might bring us to God, being put to death
in the flesh but made alive by the Spirit.*

1 PETER 3:18 NKJV

*For when we were still without strength,
in due time Christ died for the ungodly.*

ROMANS 5:6 NKJV

Today's Prayer

Dear Jesus, You are my Savior and
my protector. You suffered on the cross for me,
and I will give You honor and praise every day
of my life. I will honor You with my words,
my thoughts, and my prayers. And I will live
according to Your commandments,
so that through me, others might come
to know Your perfect love.

Amen

Devo 39

Time to Praise God

*I will praise you, Lord, with all my heart. I will tell all
the miracles you have done. I will be happy because of you;
God Most High, I will sing praises to your name.*
PSALM 9:1-2 NCV

If you're like most guys on the planet, you're a very busy
fellow. Your life is probably hectic, demanding, and
complicated. When the demands of life leave you rushing
from place to place with scarcely a moment to spare, you
may fail to pause and thank your Creator for the blessings
He has bestowed upon you. Big mistake.

No matter how busy you are, you should never be too
busy to thank God for His gifts. Your task, as an extreme
follower of the living Christ, is to praise God many times
each day. After all, your Heavenly Father has blessed you
beyond measure, and you owe Him everything, including
your thanks, starting now.

Praise opens the window of our hearts, preparing us to walk more closely with God. Prayer raises the window of our spirit, enabling us to listen more clearly to the Father.

MAX LUCADO

Be not afraid of saying too much in the praises of God; all the danger is of saying too little.

MATTHEW HENRY

Worship is an act which develops feelings for God, not a feeling for God which is expressed in an act of worship. When we obey the command to praise God in worship, our deep, essential need to be in relationship with God is nurtured.

EUGENE PETERSON

Praise him, all you people of the earth,
for he loves us with unfailing love; the faithfulnes
of the Lord endures forever. Praise the Lord!

PSALM 117 NLT

Is anyone happy?
Let him sing songs of praise.

—

JAMES 5:13 NIV

Today's Prayer

Heavenly Father, I come to You today
with hope in my heart and praise on my lips.
Make me a faithful steward of the blessings
You have entrusted to me. Let me follow in
Christ's footsteps today and every day that I
live. And let my words and deeds
praise You now and forever.
Amen

Devo 40

Not in Denial

For everyone who practices wicked things hates the light
and avoids it, so that his deeds may not be exposed.
But anyone who lives by the truth comes to the light,
so that his works may be shown to be accomplished by God.
JOHN 3:20–21 HOLMAN CSB

I f we deny our sins, we allow those sins to flourish. And if we allow sinful behaviors to become habits, we invite hardships into our own lives and into the lives of our loved ones. When we yield to the distractions and temptations of this troubled world, we suffer. But God has other intentions, and His plans for our lives do not include sin or denial.

When we allow ourselves to encounter God's presence, He will lead us away from temptation, away from confusion, and away from the self-deception. God is the champion of truth and the enemy of denial. May we see ourselves through His eyes and conduct ourselves accordingly.

There's none so blind as those who will not see.

Matthew Henry

Man prefers to believe what he prefers to be true.

Francis Bacon

What I like about experience is that it is such
an honest thing. You may take any number of
wrong turnings; but keep your eyes open and you
will not be allowed to go very far before the warning
signs appear. You may have deceived yourself,
but experience is not trying to deceive you.
The universe rings true wherever you fairly test it.

C. S. Lewis

*We justify our actions by appearances;
God examines our motives.*

Proverbs 21:2 MSG

*Buy—and do not sell—truth, wisdom,
instruction, and understanding.*

Proverbs 23:23 Holman CSB

For everyone who practices wicked things hates the light and avoids it, so that his deeds may not be exposed. But anyone who lives by the truth comes to the light, so that his works may be shown to be accomplished by God.

JOHN 3:20-21 HCSB

Today's Prayer

Dear Lord, help me see the truth,
and help me respond to the things
that I see with determination,
wisdom, and courage.

Amen

Devo 41

Big Dreams

With God's power working in us, God can do much, much more than anything we can ask or imagine.
EPHESIANS 3:20 NCV

Are you willing to entertain the possibility that God has big plans in store for you? Hopefully so. Yet sometimes, especially if you've recently experienced a life-altering disappointment, you may find it difficult to envision a brighter future for yourself and your family. If so, it's time to reconsider your own capabilities . . . and God's.

Your Heavenly Father created you with unique gifts and untapped talents; your job is to tap them. When you do, you'll begin to feel an increasing sense of confidence in yourself and in your future.

It takes courage to dream big dreams. You will discover that courage when you do three things: accept the past, trust God to handle the future, and make the most of the time He has given you today.

Nothing is too difficult for God, and no dreams are too big for Him—not even yours. So start living—and dreaming—accordingly.

Set goals so big that unless God helps you,
you will be a miserable failure.

BILL BRIGHT

To make your dream come true, you have to stay awake.

DENNIS SWANBERG

You cannot out-dream God.

JOHN ELDREDGE

*I came so they can have real and eternal life, more and
better life than they ever dreamed of.*

JOHN 10:10 MSG

Where there is no vision, the people perish . . . .

PROVERBS 29:18 KJV

*It is pleasant to see dreams come true,
but fools will not turn from evil to attain them.*

PROVERBS 13:19 NLT

Be of good courage,
and he shall strengthen your heart,
all ye that hope in the LORD.

—

Psalm 31:24 KJV

Today's Prayer

Dear Lord, give me the courage to dream and the faithfulness to trust in Your perfect plan. When I am worried or weary, give me strength for today and hope for tomorrow. Keep me mindful of Your healing power, Your infinite love, and Your eternal salvation.

Amen

Devo 42

Forgiveness Now

Then Peter came to him and asked, "Lord, how often should I forgive someone who sins against me? Seven times?" "No!" Jesus replied, "seventy times seven!"

MATTHEW 18:21-22 NLT

Are you the kind of guy who carries a grudge? If so, you know sometimes it's very tough to forgive the people who have hurt you. And that's too bad because life would be much simpler if we could forgive people "once and for all" and be done with it. But forgiveness is seldom that easy. For most of us, the decision to forgive is straightforward, but the process of forgiving is more difficult. Forgiveness is a journey that requires effort, time, perseverance, and prayer.

If there exists even one person whom you have not forgiven (and that includes yourself), follow God's commandment and His will for your life: forgive that person today. And remember that bitterness, anger, and regret are not part of God's plan for your life. Forgiveness is.

If you sincerely wish to forgive someone, pray for that person. And then pray for yourself by asking God to heal your heart. Don't expect forgiveness to be easy or quick, but rest assured: with God as your partner, you can forgive . . . and you will.

God's heart of mercy provides for us not only pardon from sin but also a daily provision of spiritual food to strengthen us.

JIM CYMBALA

There is always room for more loving forgiveness within our homes.

JAMES DOBSON

Learning how to forgive and forget is one of the secrets of a happy Christian life.

WARREN WIERSBE

Hatred stirs up trouble, but love forgives all wrongs.

PROVERBS 10:12 NCV

And whenever you stand praying, if you have anything against anyone, forgive him, so that your Father in heaven may also forgive you your wrongdoing.

MARK 11:25 HOLMAN CSB

Be even-tempered, content with second place, quick to forgive an offense. Forgive as quickly and completely as the Master forgave you. And regardless of what else you put on, wear love. It's your basic, all-purpose garment. Never be without it.

—

Colossians 3:13-14 MSG

Today's Prayer

Heavenly Father, forgiveness is Your commandment, and I know that I should forgive others just as You have forgiven me. But, genuine forgiveness is difficult. Help me to forgive those who have injured me, and deliver me from the traps of anger and bitterness. Forgiveness is Your way, Lord; let it be mine.

Amen

Devo 43

Enthused about Life

Whatever you do, do it enthusiastically,
as something done for the Lord and not for men.
COLOSSIANS 3:23 HOLMAN CSB

D o you see each day as a glorious opportunity to serve God and to do His will? Are you enthused about life, or do you struggle through each day giving scarcely a thought to God's blessings? Are you constantly praising God for His gifts, and are you sharing His Good News with the world? And are you excited about the possibilities for service that God has placed before you, whether at home, at work, at church, or at school? You should be.

You are the recipient of Christ's sacrificial love. Accept it enthusiastically and share it fervently. Jesus deserves your enthusiasm; the world deserves it; and you deserve the experience of sharing it.

Catch on fire with enthusiasm and people will come for miles to watch you burn.

JOHN WESLEY

When we wholeheartedly commit ourselves to God, there is nothing mediocre or run-of-the-mill about us. To live for Christ is to be passionate about our Lord and about our lives.

JIM GALLERY

Wherever you are, be all there. Live to the hilt every situation you believe to be the will of God.

JIM ELLIOT

Never be lazy in your work,
but serve the Lord enthusiastically.

ROMANS 12:11 NLT

Whatever work you do, do your best, because you are going to the grave, where there is no working . . . .

ECCLESIASTES 9:10 NCV

Do your work with enthusiasm.
Work as if you were serving the Lord,
not as if you were serving
only men and women.

—

EPHESIANS 6:7 NCV

Today's Prayer

Dear Lord, You have called me not to
a life of mediocrity, but to a life of passion.
Today, I will be an enthusiastic follower of
Your Son, and I will share His Good News—
and His love—with all who cross my path.
Amen

Devo 44

Excuses Everywhere

*People's own foolishness ruins their lives,
but in their minds they blame the Lord.*
PROVERBS 19:3 NCV

Excuses are everywhere . . . excellence is not. Whether you're a seasoned veteran or a wet-behind-the-ears rookie, your work is a picture book of your priorities. So whatever your job description, it's up to you, and no one else, to become masterful at your craft. It's up to you to do your job right, and to do it right now.

Because we humans are such creative excuse-makers, all of the best excuses have already been taken—we've heard them all before.

So if you're wasting your time trying to concoct a new and improved excuse, don't bother. It's impossible. A far better strategy is this: do the work. Now. Then, let your excellent work speak loudly and convincingly for itself.

Replace your excuses with fresh determination.

CHARLES SWINDOLL

An excuse is only the skin of a reason stuffed with a lie.

VANCE HAVNER

Jesus knows one of the greatest barriers to our faith is often our unwillingness to be made whole—our unwillingness to accept responsibility—our unwillingness to live without excuse for our spiritual smallness and immaturity.

ANNE GRAHAM LOTZ

Let us live in a right way . . . clothe yourselves with the Lord Jesus Christ and forget about satisfying your sinful self.

ROMANS 13:13-14 NCV

Therefore, get your minds ready for action, being self-disciplined, and set your hope completely on the grace to be brought to you at the revelation of Jesus Christ.

1 PETER 1:13 HOLMAN CSB

Be strong and courageous,
and do the work. Don't be afraid or
discouraged, for the Lord God,
my God, is with you.
He won't leave you or forsake you.

—

1 CHRONICLES 28:20 HCSB

Today's Prayer

Dear Lord, when I make a mistake, I want to
admit it. Help me not blame others for
the mistakes that I make. And when I make
a mistake, help me to learn from it.

Amen

Devo 45

Using Your Gifts

I remind you to keep ablaze the gift of God that is in you.
2 TIMOTHY 1:6 HOLMAN CSB

Face it: you've got an array of talents that need to be refined. All people possess special gifts—bestowed from the Father above—and you are no exception. But, your gift is no guarantee of success; it must be cultivated—by you—or it will go unused . . . and God's gift to you will be squandered.

Today, make a promise to yourself that you will earnestly seek to discover the talents that God has given you. Then, nourish those talents and make them grow. Finally, vow to share your gifts with the world for as long as God gives you the power to do so. After all, the best way to say "Thank You" for God's gifts is to use them.

Employ whatever God has entrusted you with,
in doing good, all possible good,
in every possible kind and degree.

JOHN WESLEY

God often reveals His direction for our lives through
the way He made us...with a certain personality
and unique skills.

BILL HYBELS

You are the only person on earth who can use your ability.

ZIG ZIGLAR

*Each one has his own gift from God,
one in this manner and another in that.*

1 CORINTHIANS 7:7 NKJV

*Every generous act and every perfect gift is from above,
coming down from the Father of lights.*

JAMES 1:17 HOLMAN CSB

Today's Prayer

Lord, I praise You for Your priceless gifts.
I give thanks for Your creation, for Your Son,
and for the unique talents and opportunities
that You have given me. Let me use my gifts
for the glory of Your kingdom,
this day and every day.
Amen

Devo 46

Too Many Distractions?

*Look straight ahead, and fix your eyes on what lies before
you. Mark out a straight path for your feet;
then stick to the path and stay safe. Don't get sidetracked;
keep your feet from following evil.*

PROVERBS 4:25-27 NLT

All of us must live through those days when the traffic jams, the computer crashes, and the dog makes a main course out of our homework. But, when we find ourselves distracted by the minor frustrations of life, we must catch ourselves, take a deep breath, and lift our thoughts upward.

Although we may, at times, struggle mightily to rise above the distractions of everyday living, we need never struggle alone. God is here—eternal and faithful, with infinite patience and love—and, if we reach out to Him, He will restore our sense of perspective and give peace to our souls.

Paul did one thing. Most of us dabble in forty things.
Are you a doer or a dabbler?

VANCE HAVNER

Only the man who follows the command of Jesus
single-mindedly and unresistingly let his yoke rest upon him,
finds his burden easy, and under its gentle pressure receives
the power to persevere in the right way.

DIETRICH BONHOEFFER

So let's keep focused on that goal [reaching out to Christ],
those of us who want everything God has for us.
If any of you have something else in mind,
something less than total commitment,
God will clear your blurred vision, you'll see it yet!

PHILIPPIANS 3:15-16 MSG

Look straight ahead, and fix your eyes on what lies before
you. Mark out a straight path for your feet;
then stick to the path and stay safe. Don't get sidetracked;
keep your feet from following evil.

PROVERBS 4:25-27 NLT

Today's Prayer

Dear Lord, help me to face this day with
a spirit of optimism and thanksgiving.
And let me focus my thoughts on You
and Your incomparable gifts.

Amen

Devo 47

You and Your Conscience

*If the way you live isn't consistent with what you believe,
then it's wrong.*
ROMANS 14:23 MSG

B illy Graham correctly observed, "Most of us follow our conscience as we follow a wheelbarrow. We push it in front of us in the direction we want to go." To do so, of course, is a profound mistake. Yet all of us, on occasion, have failed to listen to the voice that God planted in our hearts, and all of us have suffered the consequences.

God gave you a conscience for a very good reason: to make your path conform to His will. Wise believers make it a practice to listen carefully to that quiet internal voice. Count yourself among that number. When your conscience speaks, listen and learn. In all likelihood, God is trying to get His message through. And in all likelihood, it is a message that you desperately need to hear.

The beginning of backsliding means your conscience
does not answer to the truth.

OSWALD SANDERS

To go against one's conscience is neither safe nor right.
Here I stand. I cannot do otherwise.

MARTIN LUTHER

The convicting work of the Holy Spirit awakens,
disturbs, and judges.

FRANKLIN GRAHAM

*Let us draw near to God with a sincere heart in full assurance
of faith, having our hearts sprinkled to cleanse us
from a guilty conscience and having our bodies washed
with pure water.*

HEBREWS 10:22 NIV

*I will maintain my righteousness and never let go of it;
my conscience will not reproach me as long as I live.*

JOB 27:6 NIV

Create in me a pure heart, O God,
and renew a steadfast spirit within me.

—

PSALM 51:10 NIV

Today's Prayer

Dear Lord, You speak to me through the gift of Your Holy Word. And, Father, You speak to me through that still small voice that tells me right from wrong. Let me follow Your way, Lord, and, in these quiet moments, show me Your plan for this day, that I might serve You.

Amen

Devo 48

God Is Love

Unfailing love surrounds those who trust the LORD.
PSALM 32:10 NLT

The Bible makes this promise: God is love. It's a sweeping statement, a profoundly important description of what God is and how God works. God's love is perfect. When we open our hearts to His perfect love, we are touched by the Creator's hand, and we are transformed.

Today, even if you can only carve out a few quiet moments, offer sincere prayers of thanksgiving to your Creator. He loves you now and throughout all eternity. Open your heart to His presence and His love.

The life of faith is a daily exploration of the constant
and countless ways in which God's grace
and love are experienced.

EUGENE PETERSON

If you have an obedience problem, you have
a love problem. Focus your attention on God's love.

HENRY BLACKABY

Even when we cannot see the why and wherefore of
God's dealings, we know that there is love in
and behind them, so we can rejoice always.

J. I. PACKER

Praise him, all you people of the earth,
for he loves us with unfailing love;
the faithfulness of the Lord endures forever.
Praise the Lord!

PSALM 117 NLT

But God demonstrates his own love for us in this:
While we were still sinners, Christ died for us.

ROMANS 5:8 NIV

FOR GUYS

His banner over me was love.

———

Song of Solomon 2:4 KJV

Today's Prayer

Thank You, Dear God, for Your love.
You are my loving Father. I thank You for
Your love and for Your Son. I will praise You;
I will worship You; and, I will love You today,
tomorrow, and forever.

Amen

Devo 49

Beyond Fear

I sought the Lord, and He answered me
and delivered me from all my fears.

PSALM 34:4 HOLMAN CSB

We live in a world that is, at times, a frightening place. We live in a world that is, at times, a discouraging place. We live in a world where life-changing losses can be so painful and so profound that it seems we will never recover. But, with God's help, and with the help of encouraging family members and friends, we can recover.

During the darker days of life, we are wise to remember the words of Jesus, who reassured His disciples, saying, "Take courage! It is I. Don't be afraid" (Matthew 14:27 NIV). Then, with God's comfort and His love in our hearts, we can offer encouragement to others. And by helping them face their fears, we can, in turn, tackle our own problems with courage, determination, and faith.

One of the main missions of God is to free us from
the debilitating bonds of fear and anxiety.
God's heart is broken when He sees us so demoralized
and weighed down by fear.

BILL HYBELS

When we meditate on God and remember
the promises He has given us in His Word,
our faith grows, and our fears dissolve.

CHARLES STANLEY

The Lord Jesus by His Holy Spirit is with me,
and the knowledge of His presence dispels
the darkness and allays any fears.

BILL BRIGHT

For God has not given us a spirit of fear,
but of power and of love and of a sound mind.

2 TIMOTHY 1:7 NLT

Indeed, God is my salvation. I will trust [Him]
and not be afraid.

ISAIAH 12:2 HOLMAN CSB

I leave you peace; my peace I give you.
I do not give it to you as the world does.
So don't let your hearts
be troubled or afraid.

JOHN 14:27 NCV

Today's Prayer

Your Word reminds me, Lord, that even when
I walk through the valley of the shadow
of death, I need fear no evil, for You are with me,
and You comfort me. Thank You,
Lord, for a perfect love that casts out fear.
Let me live courageously and faithfully
this day and every day.

Amen

Devo 50

So Many Questions

We are pressured in every way but not crushed;
we are perplexed but not in despair.

2 CORINTHIANS 4:8 HOLMAN CSB

S o many questions and so few answers! If that statement
seems to describe the current state of your spiritual
life, don't panic. Even the most faithful Christians are
overcome by occasional bouts of fear and doubt. You are no
different.

When you feel that your faith is being tested to its limits,
seek the comfort and assurance of the One who sent His
Son as a sacrifice for you. And remember: Even when you
feel very distant from God, God is never distant from you.
When you sincerely seek His presence, He will touch your
heart, calm your fears, and restore your soul.

A prudent question is one-half of wisdom.

Francis Bacon

Be to the world a sign that while we as Christians
do not have all the answers,
we do know and care about the questions.

Billy Graham

When there is perplexity there is always guidance—
not always at the moment we ask, but in good time,
which is God's time. There is no need to fret and stew.

Elisabeth Elliot

We are pressured in every way but not crushed;
we are perplexed but not in despair.

2 Corinthians 4:8 Holman CSB

But the wisdom from above is first pure, then peace-loving,
gentle, compliant, full of mercy and good fruits,
without favoritism and hypocrisy.

James 3:17 Holman CSB

Today's Prayer

Dear Lord, when I have questions that
I can't answer, I will trust You. And I will do
my best to offer help to those who need it,
so that through me, others, too, might come
to know You and trust You.
Amen

Problem-solving 101

People who do what is right may have many problems,
but the Lord will solve them all.

PSALM 34:19 NCV

Life is an adventure in problem-solving. The question is not whether we will encounter problems; the real question is how we will choose to address them. When it comes to solving the problems of everyday living, we often know precisely what needs to be done, but we may be slow in doing it—especially if what needs to be done is difficult. So we put off till tomorrow what should be done today.

As a young man living here in the 21st century, you have your own set of challenges. As you face those challenges, you may be comforted by this fact: Trouble, of every kind, is temporary. Yet God's grace is eternal. And worries, of every kind, are temporary. But God's love is everlasting. The troubles that concern you will pass. God remains. And for every problem, God has a solution.

The words of Psalm 34 remind us that the Lord solves problems for "people who do what is right." And usually, doing "what is right" means doing the uncomfortable work of confronting our problems sooner rather than later. So with no further ado, let the problem-solving begin . . . right now.

Each problem is a God-appointed instructor.

CHARLES SWINDOLL

We are all faced with a series of great opportunities,
brilliantly disguised as unsolvable problems.
Unsolvable without God's wisdom, that is.

CHARLES SWINDOLL

Life will be made or broken at the place
where we meet and deal with obstacles.

E. STANLEY JONES

*People who do what is right may have many problems,
but the Lord will solve them all.*

PSALM 34:19 NCV

*Be joyful because you have hope.
Be patient when trouble comes,
and pray at all times.*

ROMANS 12:12 NCV

Today's Prayer

Lord, sometimes my problems are simply too big for me, but they are never too big for You. Let me turn my troubles over to You, Lord, and let me trust in You today and for all eternity.

Amen

Devo 52

Critics Beware

*Don't criticize one another, brothers. He who criticizes
a brother or judges his brother criticizes the law
and judges the law. But if you judge the law,
you are not a doer of the law but a judge.*
JAMES 4:11 HOLMAN CSB

From experience, we know that it is easier to criticize than to correct. And we know that it is easier to find faults than solutions. Yet the urge to criticize others remains a powerful temptation for most of us. Our task, as obedient believers, is to break the twin habits of negative thinking and critical speech.

Negativity is highly contagious: we give it to others who, in turn, give it back to us. This cycle can be broken by positive thoughts, heartfelt prayers, and encouraging words. As thoughtful servants of a loving God, we can use the transforming power of Christ's love to break the chains of negativity. And we should.

Being critical of others, including God,
is one way we try to avoid facing and judging our own sins.

WARREN WIERSBE

The scrutiny we give other people should be for ourselves.

OSWALD CHAMBERS

We shall never come to the perfect man
til we come to the perfect world.

MATTHEW HENRY

A man who lacks judgment derides his neighbor,
but a man of understanding holds his tongue.

PROVERBS 11:12 NIV

Our Father is kind; you be kind. Don't pick on people,
jump on their failures, criticize their faults—
unless, of course, you want the same treatment.
Don't condemn those who are down;
that hardness can boomerang.
Be easy on people; you'll find life a lot easier.

LUKE 6:36-37 MSG

So let's agree to use all our energy in
getting along with each other.
Help others with encouraging words;
don't drag them down by finding fault.

—

Romans 14:19-20 MSG

Today's Prayer

Help me, Lord, rise above the need
to criticize others. May my own shortcomings
humble me, and may I always be a source
of genuine encouragement to
my family and friends.
Amen

Devo 53

Stand Up and Be Counted

Do what God's teaching says; when you only listen and do nothing, you are fooling yourselves.

JAMES 1:22 NCV

Sometimes it's hard being a Christian, especially when the world keeps pumping out messages that are contrary to your faith.

The media is working around the clock in an attempt to rearrange your priorities. The media says that your appearance is all-important, that your clothes are all-important, that your car is all-important, and that partying is all-important. But guess what? Those messages are lies. The important things in your life have little to do with parties or appearances. The all-important things in life have to do with your faith, your family, and your future. Period.

So do yourself a favor: forget the media hype, and pay attention to God. Stand up for Him and be counted, not just in church where it's relatively easy to be a Christian, but also outside the church, where it's significantly harder. You owe it God . . . and you owe it to yourself.

God calls us to be committed to Him,
to be committed to making a difference,
and to be committed to reconciliation.

BILL HYBELS

Once you have thoroughly examined your values
and articulated them, you will be able to
steer your life by them.

JOHN MAXWELL

Believe and do what God says.
The life-changing consequences will be limitless,
and the results will be confidence and peace of mind.

FRANKLIN GRAHAM

*Everyone who believes that Jesus is the Messiah
has been born of God, and everyone who loves
the parent also loves his child.*

1 JOHN 5:1 HOLMAN CSB

*I know whom I have believed and am persuaded
that He is able to guard what has been
entrusted to me until that day.*

2 TIMOTHY 1:12 HOLMAN CSB

Then Jesus told the centurion,
"Go. As you have believed,
let it be done for you." And his servant
was cured that very moment.

—

Matthew 8:13 HCSB

Today's Prayer

Heavenly Father, I believe in You, and I believe
in Your Word. Help me to live in such
a way that my actions validate my beliefs—
and let the glory be Yours forever.
Amen

Devo 54

The Right Kind of Fear

*A simple life in the Fear-of-God is better
than a rich life with a ton of headaches.*
PROVERBS 15:16 MSG

God's hand shapes the universe, and it shapes our lives. God maintains absolute sovereignty over His creation, and His power is beyond comprehension. As believers, we must cultivate a sincere respect for God's awesome power. God has dominion over all things, and until we acknowledge His sovereignty, we lack the humility we need to live righteously, and we lack the humility we need to become wise.

The fear of the Lord is, indeed, the beginning of knowledge. So today, as you face the realities of everyday life, remember this: until you acquire a healthy, respectful fear of God's power, your education is incomplete, and so is your faith.

A healthy fear of God will do much to deter us from sin.

CHARLES SWINDOLL

The remarkable thing about fearing God is that when you fear God, you fear nothing else, whereas if you do not fear God, you fear everything else.

OSWALD CHAMBERS

When true believers are awed by the greatness of God and by the privilege of becoming His children, then they become sincerely motivated, effective evangelists.

BILL HYBELS

Don't consider yourself to be wise;
fear the Lord and turn away from evil.

PROVERBS 3:7 HOLMAN CSB

The fear of the Lord is the beginning of wisdom;
all who follow His instructions have good insight.

PSALM 111:10 HOLMAN CSB

Honor all people. Love the brotherhood.
Fear God. Honor the king.

—

1 PETER 2:17 NKJV

Today's Prayer

Lord, You love me and protect me.
I praise You, Father, for Your grace,
and I respect You for Your infinite power.
Let my greatest fear in life be the fear of
displeasing You.
Amen

Devo 55

Answering the Call

God chose you to be his people,
so I urge you now to live the life to which God called you.

EPHESIANS 4:1 NCV

t is vitally important that you heed God's call. In John 15:16, Jesus says, "You did not choose me, but I chose you and appointed you to go and bear fruit—fruit that will last" (NIV). In other words, you have been called by Christ, and now, it is up to you to decide precisely how you will answer.

Have you already found your special calling? If so, you're a very lucky guy. If not, keep searching and keep praying until you discover it. And remember this: God has important work for you to do—work that no one else on earth can accomplish but you.

When you become consumed by God's call on your life,
everything will take on new meaning and significance.
You will begin to see every facet of your life,
including your pain, as a means through which God can
work to bring others to Himself.

CHARLES STANLEY

The world does not consider labor a blessing, therefore
it flees and hates it, but the pious who fear the Lord labor
with a ready and cheerful heart, for they know
God's command, and they acknowledge His calling.

MARTIN LUTHER

*I pray that the eyes of your heart may be enlightened so you
may know what is the hope of His calling, what are
the glorious riches of His inheritance among the saints, and
what is the immeasurable greatness of His power to us who
believe, according to the working of His vast strength.*

EPHESIANS 1:18-19 HOLMAN CSB

*So the last shall be first, and the first last:
for many be called, but few chosen.*

MATTHEW 20:16 KJV

One thing I do, forgetting those things
which are behind and reaching forward
to those things which are ahead,
I press toward the goal for the prize
of the upward call of God in Christ Jesus.

—

PHILIPPIANS 3:13-14 NKJV

Today's Prayer

Heavenly Father, You have called me, and
I acknowledge that calling. In these quiet
moments before this busy day unfolds,
I come to You. I will study Your Word
and seek Your guidance. Give me the wisdom
to know Your will for my life and the courage
to follow wherever You may lead me,
today and forever.

Amen

Devo 56

God's Promises

Let us hold on to the confession of our hope without wavering, for He who promised is faithful.

HEBREWS 10:23 HOLMAN CSB

God has made quite a few promises to you, and He intends to keep every single one of them. You will find these promises in a book like no other: the Holy Bible. The Bible is your roadmap for life here on earth and for life eternal—as a believer, you are called upon to trust its promises, to follow its commandments, and to share its Good News.

God has made promises to all of humanity and to you. God's promises never fail and they never grow old. You must trust those promises and share them with your family, with your friends, and with the world . . . starting now . . . and ending never.

God's promises are overflowings from his great heart.

C. H. SPURGEON

There are four words I wish we would never forget,
and they are, "God keeps his word."

CHARLES SWINDOLL

The stars may fall, but God's promises will stand
and be fulfilled.

J. I. PACKER

*Patient endurance is what you need now,
so you will continue to do God's will.
Then you will receive all that he has promised.*

HEBREWS 10:36 NLT

*Whatever God has promised gets stamped with
the Yes of Jesus. In him, this is what we preach and pray,
the great Amen, God's Yes and our Yes together,
gloriously evident.*

2 CORINTHIANS 1:20 MSG

What time I am afraid,
I will trust in thee.

—

PSALM 56:3 KJV

Today's Prayer

Lord, Your Holy Word contains promises, and
I will trust them. I will use the Bible as my
guide, and I will trust You, Lord, to speak to me
through Your Holy Spirit and through
Your Holy Word, this day and forever.

Amen

Devo 57

Talking Behind Their Backs

*If anyone considers himself religious and yet
does not keep a tight rein on his tongue,
he deceives himself and his religion is worthless.*

JAMES 1:26 NIV

Face it: gossip is bad—and the Bible clearly tells us that gossip is wrong. When we say things that we don't want other people to know we said, we're being somewhat dishonest, but if the things we say aren't true, we're being very dishonest. Either way, we have done something that we may regret later, especially when the other person finds out.

So do yourself a big favor: don't gossip. It's a waste of words, and it's the wrong thing to do. You'll feel better about yourself if you don't gossip (and other people will feel better about you, too). So don't do it!

Change the heart, and you change the speech.

WARREN WIERSBE

I still believe we ought to talk about Jesus.
The old country doctor of my boyhood days always began
his examination by saying, "Let me see your tongue."
That's a good way to check a Christian: the tongue test.
Let's hear what he is talking about.

VANCE HAVNER

The great test of a man's character is his tongue.

OSWALD CHAMBERS

Though some tongues just love the taste of gossip,
Christians have better uses for language than that.
Don't talk dirty or silly. That kind of talk doesn't fit our style.
Thanksgiving is our dialect.

EPHESIANS 5:4 MSG

Stay calm; mind your own business; do your own job.
You've heard all this from us before,
but a reminder never hurts.

1 THESSALONIANS 4:11 MSG

If you really carry out the royal law
prescribed in Scripture,
You shall love your neighbor as yourself,
you are doing well.

JAMES 2:8 HCSB

Today's Prayer

Lord, You have warned me that I will be judged by the words I speak. And, You have commanded me to choose my words carefully so that I might be a source of encouragement and hope to my family and to the world. Let the words that I speak today be worthy of the One who has saved me forever.

Amen

Devo 58

He's Here

I am not alone, because the Father is with Me.
JOHN 16:32 HOLMAN CSB

Do you ever wonder if God really hears your prayers? If so, you're in good company: lots of very faithful Christians have wondered the same thing. In fact, some of the biggest heroes in the Bible had their doubts—and so, perhaps, will you. But when you have your doubts, remember this: God isn't on vacation, and He hasn't moved out of town. God isn't taking a coffee break, and He isn't snoozing on the couch. He's right here, right now, listening to your thoughts and prayers, watching over your every move.

As the demands of everyday life weigh down upon you, you may be tempted to ignore God's presence or—worse yet—to rebel against His commandments. But, when you quiet yourself and acknowledge His presence, God touches your heart and restores your spirits. So why not let Him do it right now?

Get yourself into the presence of the loving Father.
Just place yourself before Him, and look up into, His face;
think of His love, His wonderful, tender, pitying love.

ANDREW MURRAY

There is a basic urge: the longing for unity.
You desire a reunion with God—with God your Father.

E. STANLEY JONES

The next time you hear a baby laugh or see an ocean wave,
take note. Pause and listen as his Majesty whispers
ever so gently, "I'm here."

MAX LUCADO

*Surely goodness and mercy shall follow me
all the days of my life: and I will dwell
in the house of the Lord for ever.*

PSALM 23:6 KJV

Draw near to God, and He will draw near to you.

JAMES 4:8 HOLMAN CSB

You will seek Me and find Me when you
search for Me with all your heart.

—

Jeremiah 29:13 HCSB

Today's Prayer

Dear Lord, You are with me always.
Help me feel Your presence in every situation
and every circumstance. Today, Dear God,
let me feel You and acknowledge Your presence,
Your love, and Your Son.
Amen

Devo 59

A Rule That's Golden

Do to others as you would have them do to you.
LUKE 6:31 NIV

Is the Golden Rule your rule, or is it just another Bible verse that goes in one ear and out the other? Jesus made Himself perfectly clear: He instructed you to treat other people in the same way that you want to be treated. But sometimes, especially when you're feeling pressure from friends, or when we're tired or upset, obeying the Golden Rule can seem like an impossible task—but it's not.

God wants each of us to treat other people with respect, kindness, and courtesy. He wants us to rise above our own imperfections, and He wants us to treat others with unselfishness and love. To make it short and sweet, God wants us to obey the Golden Rule, and He knows we can do it.

So if you're wondering how to treat someone else, ask the person you see every time you look into the mirror. The answer you receive will tell you exactly what to do.

Faith never asks whether good works are to be done,
but has done them before there is time to ask the question,
and it is always doing them.

MARTIN LUTHER

The mark of a Christian is that he will walk the second mile
and turn the other cheek. A wise man or woman gives
the extra effort, all for the glory of the Lord Jesus Christ.

JOHN MAXWELL

When you extend hospitality to others, you're not trying to
impress people, you're trying to reflect God to them.

MAX LUCADO

*Let us not become weary in doing good,
for at the proper time we will reap a harvest
if we do not give up.*

GALATIANS 6:9 NIV

*Each of you should look not only to your own interests,
but also to the interest of others.*

PHILIPPIANS 2:4 NIV

Today's Prayer

Dear Lord, let me treat others as I wish to be
treated. Because I expect kindness,
let me be kind. Because I wish to be loved,
let me be loving. Because I need forgiveness,
let me be merciful. In all things, Lord,
let me live by the Golden Rule, and let me teach
that rule to others through my words
and my deeds.
Amen

Devo 60

Time for Fun

So I recommend having fun, because there is nothing better for people to do in this world than to eat, drink, and enjoy life. That way they will experience some happiness along with all the hard work God gives them.

ECCLESIASTES 8:15 NLT

Are you a guy who takes time each day to really enjoy life? Hopefully so. After all, you are the recipient of a precious gift—the gift of life. And because God has seen fit to give you this gift, it is incumbent upon you to use it and to enjoy it. But sometimes, amid the inevitable pressures of everyday living, really enjoying life may seem almost impossible. It is not.

For most of us, fun is as much a function of attitude as it is a function of environment. So whether you're standing victorious atop one of life's mountains or trudging through one of life's valleys, enjoy yourself. You deserve to have fun today, and God wants you to have fun today . . . so what on earth are you waiting for?

FOR GUYS

The happiest people in the world are not those who have
no problems, but the people who have learned to live
with those things that are less than perfect.

JAMES DOBSON

If we don't hunger and thirst after righteousness,
we'll become anemic and feel miserable in
our Christian experience.

FRANKLIN GRAHAM

True happiness and contentment cannot come from the
things of this world. The blessedness of true joy is a free gift
that comes only from our Lord and Savior, Jesus Christ.

DENNIS SWANBERG

Make me to hear joy and gladness.
PSALM 51:8 KJV

Thou wilt show me the path of life:
in thy presence is fulness of joy; at thy right hand there
are pleasures for evermore.
PSALM 16:11 KJV

Today's Prayer

Dear Lord, You are my strength and my joy. I will rejoice in the day that You have made, and I will give thanks for the countless blessings that You have given me. Let me be a joyful Christian, Father, as I share the Good News of Your Son, and let me praise You for all the marvelous things You have done.

Amen

Devo 61

A Happy Christian

Happy are the people whose strength is in You,
whose hearts are set on pilgrimage.
PSALM 84:5 HOLMAN CSB

Happiness depends less upon our circumstances than upon our thoughts. When we turn our thoughts to God, to His gifts, and to His glorious creation, we experience the joy that God intends for His children. But, when we focus on the negative aspects of life, we suffer needlessly.

Do you sincerely want to be a happy Christian? Then set your mind and your heart upon God's love and His grace. The fullness of life in Christ is available to all who seek it and claim it. Count yourself among that number. Seek first the salvation that is available through a personal relationship with Jesus Christ, and then claim the joy, the peace, and the spiritual abundance that the Shepherd offers His sheep.

Whoever possesses God is happy.

St. Augustine

There is no correlation between wealth and happiness.

Larry Burkett

Our thoughts, not our circumstances,
determine our happiness.

John Maxwell

A cheerful heart is good medicine....

Proverbs 17:22 NIV

*I will praise you, Lord, with all my heart. I will tell all
the miracles you have done. I will be happy because of you;
God Most High, I will sing praises to your name.*

Psalm 9:1-2 NCV

*But happy are those . . .
whose hope is in the LORD their God.*

Psalm 146:5 NLT

I've learned by now to be quite content
whatever my circumstances.
I'm just as happy with little as with
much, with much as with little.
I've found the recipe for being happy
whether full or hungry,
hands full or hands empty.

PHILIPPIANS 4:11-12 MSG

Today's Prayer

Lord, make me a happy Christian.
Let me rejoice in the gift of this day,
and let me praise You for the gift of Your Son.
Make me be a joyful person, Lord, as I share
Your Good News with all those who need
Your healing touch.
Amen

Devo 62

What a Friend

Therefore if any man be in Christ, he is a new creature:
old things are passed away; behold,
all things are become new.

2 CORINTHIANS 5:17 KJV

Our circumstances change but Jesus does not. Even when the world seems to be trembling between our feet, Jesus remains the spiritual bedrock that cannot be moved.

The old familiar hymn begins, "What a friend we have in Jesus...." No truer words were ever penned. Jesus is the sovereign Friend and ultimate Savior of mankind. Christ showed enduring love for His believers by willingly sacrificing His own life so that we might have eternal life. Let us love Him, praise Him, and share His message of salvation with our neighbors and with the world.

Jesus was the perfect reflection of God's nature in
every situation He encountered during
His time here on earth.

BILL HYBELS

Jesus came into the world so we could know,
once and for all, that God is concerned about the way we
live, the way we believe, and the way we die.

BILLY GRAHAM

Jesus: the proof of God's love.

PHILIP YANCEY

Jesus Christ is the same yesterday, today, and forever.

HEBREWS 13:8 HOLMAN CSB

*But we do see Jesus—made lower than the angels
for a short time so that by God's grace He might taste death
for everyone—crowned with glory and honor because
of the suffering of death.*

HEBREWS 2:9 HOLMAN CSB

I have come as a light into the world,
so that everyone who believes in Me
would not remain in darkness.

—

JOHN 12:46 HCSB

Today's Prayer

Heavenly Father, I praise You for Your Son. Jesus is my Savior and my strength. Let me share His Good News with all who cross my path, and let me share His love with all who need His healing touch.

Amen

Devo 63

Obedience Now

*Not everyone who says to Me, "Lord, Lord!" will enter
the kingdom of heaven, but the one who does
the will of My Father in heaven.*

MATTHEW 7:21 HOLMAN CSB

God's commandments are not "suggestions," and they are not "helpful hints." They are, instead, immutable laws which, if followed, lead to repentance, salvation, and abundance. But if you choose to disobey the commandments of your Heavenly Father or the teachings of His Son, you will most surely reap a harvest of regret.

The formula for a successful life is surprisingly straightforward: Study God's Word and obey it. Does this sound too simple? Perhaps it is simple, but it is also the only way to reap the marvelous riches that God has in store for you.

Obedience is the outward expression of your love of God.

HENRY BLACKABY

Believe and do what God says. The life-changing consequences will be limitless, and the results will be confidence and peace of mind.

FRANKLIN GRAHAM

All true knowledge of God is born out of obedience.

JOHN CALVIN

Those who obey his commands live in him,
and he in them. And this is how we know that he lives in us:
We know it by the Spirit he gave us.

1 JOHN 3:24 NIV

You shall walk after the Lord your God and fear Him,
and keep His commandments and obey His voice,
and you shall serve Him and hold fast to Him.

DEUTERONOMY 13:4 NKJV

If they obey and serve him,
they will spend the rest of their days
in prosperity and their years
in contentment.

—

JOB 36:11 NIV

Today's Prayer

Heavenly Father, when I turn my thoughts
away from You and Your Word, I suffer.
But when I obey Your commandments,
when I place my faith in You, I am secure.
Let me live according to Your commandments.
Direct my path far from the temptations
and distractions of this world.
And, let me discover Your will and follow it,
Dear Lord, this day and always.
Amen

Devo 64

You and Your Family

...these should learn first of all to put their religion into practice by caring for their own family....

1 TIMOTHY 5:4 NIV

D o you sometimes take your family for granted? If so, welcome to the club. At time, it's surprisingly easy to ignore the people we love the most. After all, we know that they'll still love us no matter what we do. But whenever we ignore our loved ones, we're doing a big disservice to our loved ones and to ourselves.

A loving family is a treasure from God. If God has blessed you with a close knit, supportive clan, offer a word of thanks to your Creator because He has given you one of His most precious earthly possessions. Your obligation, in response to God's gift, is to treat your family in ways that are consistent with His commandments.

So the next time your family life becomes a little stressful, remember this: That little band of men, women, kids, and babies is a priceless treasure on temporary loan from the Father above. And it's your responsibility to praise God for that gift—and to act accordingly.

The only true source of meaning in life is found in love for God and his son Jesus Christ, and love for mankind, beginning with our own families.

JAMES DOBSON

It is a reverent thing to see an ancient castle or building not in decay, or to see a fair timber tree sound and perfect. How much more beautiful it is to behold an ancient and noble family that has stood against the waves and weathers of time.

FRANCIS BACON

Never give your family the leftovers and crumbs of your time.

CHARLES SWINDOLL

You must choose for yourselves today whom you will serve . . . as for me and my family, we will serve the Lord.

JOSHUA 24:15 NCV

Every kingdom divided against itself will be ruined, and every city or household divided against itself will not stand.

MATTHEW 12:25 NIV

He who brings trouble on his family
will inherit only wind....

—

PROVERBS 11:29 NIV

Today's Prayer

Dear Lord, I am part of Your family, and I praise You for Your gifts and Your love. Father, You have also blessed me with my earthly family. Let me show love and acceptance for my own family so that through me, they might come to know You.

Amen

Devo 65

Sharing Your Faith

*But sanctify the Lord God in your hearts, and always be
ready to give a defense to everyone who asks you
a reason for the hope that is in you.*

1 PETER 3:15 HOLMAN CSB

A good way to build your faith is by talking about it—
and that's precisely what God wants you to do. In his
second letter to Timothy, Paul shares a message to
believers of every generation when he writes, "God has not
given us a spirit of timidity" (1:7). Paul's meaning is clear:
When sharing your testimony, you must be courageous and
unashamed.

Let's face facts: You live in a world that desperately
needs the healing message of Jesus Christ. Every believer,
including you, bears responsibility for sharing the Good
News. And it is important to remember that you give your
testimony through your words and your actions.

So today, preach the Gospel through your words and
your deeds…but not necessarily in that order.

The sermon of your life in tough times ministers to people
more powerfully than the most eloquent speaker.

BILL BRIGHT

To take up the cross means that you take your stand for
the Lord Jesus no matter what it costs.

BILLY GRAHAM

To stand in an uncaring world and say,
"See, here is the Christ" is a daring act of courage.

CALVIN MILLER

*For God has not given us a spirit of fear and timidity,
but of power, love, and self-discipline. So you must never be
ashamed to tell others about our Lord.*

2 TIMOTHY 1:7-8 NLT

*And I say to you, anyone who acknowledges Me before men,
the Son of Man will also acknowledge him before
the angels of God; but whoever denies Me before men
will be denied before the angels of God.*

LUKE 12:8-9 HOLMAN CSB

This and this only has been
my appointed work: getting this news
to those who have never heard of God,
and explaining how it works
by simple faith and plain truth.

—

1 TIMOTHY 2:7 MSG

Today's Prayer

Dear Lord, You sent Your Son Jesus to die on a cross for me. Jesus endured indignity, suffering, and death so that I might live. Because He lives, I, too, have Your promise of eternal life. Let me share this Good News, Lord, with a world that so desperately needs Your healing hand and the salvation of Your Son. Today, let me share the message of Jesus Christ through my words and my deeds.

Amen

Devo 66

The Wisdom to Be Humble

God has chosen you and made you his holy people.
He loves you. So always do these things: Show mercy
to others, be kind, humble, gentle, and patient.
COLOSSIANS 3:12 NCV

Humility is not, in most cases, a naturally occurring human trait. Most of us, it seems, are more than willing to overestimate our own accomplishments. We are tempted to say, "Look how wonderful I am!" . . . hoping all the while that the world will agree with our own self-appraisals. But those of us who fall prey to the sin of pride should beware—God is definitely not impressed by our prideful proclamations.

God honors humility . . . and He rewards those who humbly serve Him. So if you've acquired the wisdom to be humble, then you are to be congratulated. But if you've not yet overcome the tendency to overestimate your own accomplishments, then God still has some important (and perhaps painful) lessons to teach you—lessons about humility that you still need to learn.

Humility is not thinking less of yourself;
it is thinking of yourself less.

RICK WARREN

God exalts humility. When God works in our lives,
helping us to become humble, he gives us a permanent joy.
Humility gives us a joy that cannot be taken away.

MAX LUCADO

It was pride that changed angels into devils;
it is humility that makes men as angels.

ST. AUGUSTINE

*Clothe yourselves with humility toward one another,
because God resists the proud,
but gives grace to the humble.*

1 PETER 5:5 HOLMAN CSB

*But He said to me, "My grace is sufficient for you,
for power is perfected in weakness." Therefore, I will most
gladly boast all the more about my weaknesses,
so that Christ's power may reside in me.*

2 CORINTHIANS 12:9 HOLMAN CSB

Do nothing out of rivalry or conceit,
but in humility consider others as more
important than yourselves.

—

PHILIPPIANS 2:3 HCSB

Today's Prayer

Heavenly Father, Jesus clothed Himself with humility when He chose to leave heaven and come to earth to live and die for us, His children. Christ is my Master and my example. Clothe me with humility, Lord, so that I might be more like Your Son, and keep me mindful that You are the giver and sustainer of life, and to You, Dear Lord, goes the glory and the praise.

Amen

Devo 67

Watching the Donut

I can do everything through him that gives me strength.
PHILIPPIANS 4:13 NIV

On the wall of a little donut shop, the sign said: As you travel through life, brother, whatever be your goal, keep your eye upon the donut, and not upon the hole.

Are you a Christian who keeps your eye upon the donut, or have you acquired the bad habit of looking only at the hole? Hopefully, you spend most of your waking hours looking at the donut (and thanking God for it).

Christianity and pessimism don't mix. So do yourself a favor: choose to be a hope-filled Christian. Think optimistically about your life and your future. Trust your hopes, not your fears. Take time to celebrate God's glorious creation. And then, when you've filled your heart with hope and gladness, share your optimism with your friends. They'll be better for it, and so will you. But not necessarily in that order.

Keep your feet on the ground, but let your heart soar
as high as it will. Refuse to be average or to surrender to
the chill of your spiritual environment.

A. W. TOZER

The people whom I have seen succeed best in life have
always been cheerful and hopeful people who went about
their business with a smile on their faces.

CHARLES KINGSLEY

The essence of optimism is that it takes no account of
the present, but it is a source of inspiration,
of vitality, and of hope. Where others have resigned,
it enables a man to hold his head high,
to claim the future for himself,
and not abandon it to his enemy.

DIETRICH BONHOEFFER

But if we hope for what we do not see,
we eagerly wait for it with patience.
ROMANS 8:25 HOLMAN CSB

For God has not given us a spirit of fearfulness,
but one of power, love, and sound judgment.
2 TIMOTHY 1:7 HOLMAN CSB

My cup runs over.
Surely goodness and mercy
shall follow me all the days of my life;
and I will dwell in the house
of the Lord Forever.

—

PSALM 23:5-6 NKJV

Today's Prayer

Lord, let me be an expectant Christian.
Let me expect the best from You, and let me look
for the best in others. If I become discouraged,
Father, turn my thoughts and my prayers to
You. Let me trust You, Lord, to direct my life.
And, let me share my faith and optimism with
others, today and every day that I live.

Amen

Devo 68

Peer Pressure 101

We must obey God rather than men.
ACTS 5:29 HOLMAN CSB

Rick Warren observed, "Those who follow the crowd usually get lost in it." We know those words to be true, but oftentimes we fail to live by them. Instead of trusting God for guidance, we imitate our friends and suffer the consequences. Instead of seeking to please our Father in heaven, we strive to please our peers, with decidedly mixed results. Instead of doing the right thing, we do the "easy" thing or the "popular" thing. And when we do, we pay a high price for our shortsightedness.

Would you like a time-tested formula for successful living? Here is a simple formula that is proven and true: don't give in to peer pressure. Period.

Instead of getting lost in the crowd, you should find guidance from God. Does this sound too simple? Perhaps it is simple, but it is also the only way to reap all the marvelous riches that God has in store for you.

Do you want to be wise? Choose wise friends.

CHARLES SWINDOLL

Those who follow the crowd usually get lost in it.

RICK WARREN

People who constantly, and fervently, seek the approval of others live with an identity crisis. They don't know who they are, and they are defined by what others think of them.

CHARLES STANLEY

My son, if sinners entice you, don't be persuaded.

PROVERBS 1:10 HOLMAN CSB

Blessed is the man who walks not in the counsel of the ungodly, nor stands in the path of sinners, nor sits in the seat of the scornful; but his delight is in the law of the Lord, and in His law he meditates day and night.

PSALM 1:1-2 NKJV

Today's Prayer

Dear Lord, other people may encourage me to
stray from Your path, but I wish to follow
in the footsteps of Your Son. Give me the vision
to see the right path—and the wisdom
to follow it—today and every day
of my life.
Amen

Fitness Matters

Whatever you eat or drink or whatever you do,
you must do all for the glory of God.

1 CORINTHIANS 10:31 NLT

A re you shaping up or spreading out? Do you eat sensibly and exercise regularly, or do you spend most of your time on the couch with a Twinkie in one hand and a clicker in the other? Are you choosing to treat your body like a temple or a trash heap? How you answer these questions will help determine how long you live and how well you live.

Physical fitness is a choice, a choice that requires discipline—it's as simple as that. So, do yourself this favor: treat your body like a one-of-a-kind gift from God . . . because that's precisely what your body is.

A Christian should no more defile his body
than a Jew would defile the temple.

WARREN WIERSBE

If you desire to improve your physical well-being
and your emotional outlook,
increasing your faith can help you.

JOHN MAXWELL

Jesus Christ is the One by Whom, for Whom,
through Whom everything was made. Therefore,
He knows what's wrong in your life and how to fix it.

ANNE GRAHAM LOTZ

*A cheerful disposition is good for your health;
gloom and doom leave you bone-tired.*

PROVERBS 17:22 MSG

*They brought unto him all sick people that were taken
with diverse diseases and torments . . . and he healed them.*

MATTHEW 4:24 KJV

Today's Prayer

Dear Lord, my body is Your temple—
I will treat it with care.

Amen

Devo 70

The Right Path

The LORD says, "I will guide you along the best pathway for your life. I will advise you and watch over you."

PSALM 32:8 NLT

What does God require of us? That we worship Him only, that we welcome His Son into our hearts, and that we walk humbly with our Creator. When Jesus was tempted by Satan, the Master's response was unambiguous. Jesus chose to worship the Lord and serve Him only. We, as followers of Christ, must follow in His footsteps.

When we place God in a position of secondary importance, we do ourselves great harm and we put ourselves at great risk. But when we place God squarely in the center of our lives—when we walk humbly and obediently with Him—we are blessed and we are protected.

God often keeps us on the path by guiding us through the counsel of friends and trusted spiritual advisors.

BILL HYBELS

To walk out of His will is to walk into nowhere.

C. S. LEWIS

Only by walking with God can we hope to find the path that leads to life.

JOHN ELDREDGE

And you shall do what is right and good in the sight of the Lord, that it may be well with you.

DEUTERONOMY 6:18 NKJV

Flee from youthful passions, and pursue righteousness, faith, love, and peace, along with those who call on the Lord from a pure heart.

2 TIMOTHY 2:22 HOLMAN CSB

For the eyes of the Lord are on
the righteous, and His ears are open to
their prayers; but the face of the Lord is
against those who do evil.

1 PETER 3:12 NKJV

Today's Prayer

Lord, sometimes life is difficult.
But even when I can't see any hope for
the future, You are always with me. And, I can
live courageously because I know that You
are leading me to a place where I can
accomplish Your kingdom's work . . .
and where You lead, I will follow.

Amen

Devo 71

Real Repentance

The one who conceals his sins will not prosper, but whoever confesses and renounces them will find mercy.

PROVERBS 28:13 HOLMAN CSB

Who among us has sinned? All of us. But, God calls upon us to turn away from sin by following His commandments. And the good news is this: When we do ask God's forgiveness and turn our hearts to Him, He forgives us absolutely and completely.

Genuine repentance requires more than simply offering God apologies for our misdeeds. Real repentance may start with feelings of sorrow and remorse, but it ends only when we turn away from the sin that has heretofore distanced us from our Creator. In truth, we offer our most meaningful apologies to God, not with our words, but with our actions. As long as we are still engaged in sin, we may be "repenting," but we have not fully "repented."

Is there an aspect of your life that is distancing you from your God? If so, ask for His forgiveness, and—just as importantly—stop sinning. Then, wrap yourself in the protection of God's Word. When you do, you will be secure.

Ten thousand confessions, if they do not spring from really contrite hearts, shall only be additions to their guilt.

C. H. SPURGEON

But suppose we do sin. Suppose we slip and fall. Suppose we yield to temptation for a moment. What happens? We have to confess that sin.

BILLY GRAHAM

Repentance begins with confession of our guilt and recognition that our sin is against God.

CHARLES STANLEY

If we say, "We have no sin," we are deceiving ourselves, and the truth is not in us. If we confess our sins, He is faithful and righteous to forgive us our sins and to cleanse us from all unrighteousness.

1 JOHN 1:8-9 HOLMAN CSB

There will be more joy in heaven over one sinner who repents than over 99 righteous people who don't need repentance.

LUKE 15:7 HOLMAN CSB

Fools mock at making restitution,
but there is goodwill among the upright.

———

PROVERBS 14:9 HCSB

Today's Prayer

When I stray from Your commandments, Lord,
I must not only confess my sins, I must also
turn from them. When I fall short, help me to
change. When I reject Your Word and Your will
for my life, guide me back to Your side. Forgive
my sins, Dear Lord, and help me live according
to Your plan for my life. Your plan is perfect,
Father; I am not. Let me trust in You.

Amen

Devo 72

Time for God

Don't burn out; keep yourselves fueled and aflame.
Be alert servants of the Master, cheerfully expectant.
Don't quit in hard times; pray all the harder.

ROMANS 12:11-12 MSG

How much time do you spend getting to know God? A lot? A little? Almost none? The answer to this question will determine, to a surprising extent, the state of your spiritual health. And make no mistake: the more time and energy you invest with God, the better you'll come to know Him.

God loved this world so much that He sent His Son to save it. And now only one real question remains for you: what will you do in response to God's love? The answer should be obvious: God must come first in your life. He is the Giver of all good things, and He is the One who sent His Son so that you might have eternal life. He deserves your prayers, your obedience, your stewardship, and your love—and He deserves these things all day every day, not just on Sunday mornings.

This is a day when we are so busy doing everything
that we have no time to be anything.
Even religiously we are so occupied with activities that
we have no time to know God.

VANCE HAVNER

Busyness is the great enemy of relationships.

RICK WARREN

Being busy, in and of itself, is not a sin. But being busy in
an endless pursuit of things that leave us empty and hollow
and broken inside—that cannot be pleasing to God.

MAX LUCADO

The intense prayer of the righteous is very powerful.

JAMES 5:16 HOLMAN CSB

*Let the words of my mouth and the meditation
of my heart be acceptable in Your sight, O Lord,
my strength and my Redeemer.*

PSALM 19:14 NKJV

Yet He often withdrew
to deserted places and prayed.

—

LUKE 5:16 HCSB

Today's Prayer

Dear Lord, sometimes, I am distracted
by the busyness of the day or the demands of
the moment. When I am worried or anxious,
Father, turn my thoughts back to You.
Help me to trust Your will, to follow
Your commands, and to accept Your peace,
today and forever.
Amen

Devo 73

Your Own Worst Critic?

*Those who wait for perfect weather will never plant seeds;
those who look at every cloud will never harvest crops . . . .
Plant early in the morning, and work until evening,
because you don't know if this or that will succeed.
They might both do well.*

ECCLESIASTES 11:4,6 NCV

When God made you, He equipped you with an array of talents and abilities that are uniquely yours. It's up to you to discover those talents and to use them, but sometimes your own perfectionism may get in the way.

If you're your own worst critic, give it up. After all, God doesn't expect you to be perfect, and if that's okay with Him, then it should be okay with you, too.

When you accepted Christ as your Savior, God accepted you for all eternity. Now, it's your turn to accept yourself. When you do, you'll feel a tremendous weight being lifted from your shoulders. And that's as it should be. After all, only one earthly being ever lived life to perfection, and He was the Son of God. The rest of us have fallen short of God's standard and need to be accepting of our own limitations as well as the limitations of others.

The happiest people in the world are not those
who have no problems, but the people who have learned
to live with those things that are less than perfect.

JAMES DOBSON

I want you to remember what a difference there is between
perfection and perfectionism. The former is a Bible truth;
the latter may or may not be a human perversion of
the truth. I fear that many, in their horror of
perfectionism, reject perfection too.

ANDREW MURRAY

*A devout life does bring wealth,
but it's the rich simplicity of being yourself before God.*

1 TIMOTHY 6:6 MSG

*How happy are those whose way is blameless,
who live according to the law of the Lord!
Happy are those who keep His decrees and seek Him
with all their heart.*

PSALM 119:1-2 HOLMAN CSB

To acquire wisdom is to love oneself;
people who cherish understanding
will prosper.

—

PROVERBS 19:8 NLT

Today's Prayer

Lord, this world has so many expectations of
me, but today I will not seek to meet
the world's expectations; I will do my best
to meet Your expectations. I will make You
my ultimate priority, Lord, by serving You,
by praising You, by loving You,
and by obeying You.

Amen

Devo 74

The Ultimate Armor

If God is for us, who is against us?
ROMANS 8:31 HOLMAN CSB

God has promised to protect us, and He intends to keep His promise. In a world filled with dangers and temptations, God is the ultimate armor. In a world filled with misleading messages, God's Word is the ultimate truth. In a world filled with more frustrations than we can count, God's Son offers the ultimate peace.

Will you accept God's peace and wear God's armor against the dangers of our world? Hopefully so—because when you do, you can live courageously, knowing that you possess the ultimate protection: God's unfailing love for you.

A mighty fortress is our God, a bulwark never failing.
Our helper He, amid the flood of mortal ills prevailing.
For still our ancient foe doth seek to work us woe.
His craft and power are great, armed with cruel hate,
Our earth is not his equal.

MARTIN LUTHER

The Rock of Ages is the great sheltering encirclement.

OSWALD CHAMBERS

Under heaven's lock and key, we are protected by the most
efficient security system available: the power of God.

CHARLES SWINDOLL

*He giveth power to the faint; and to them that have
no might he increaseth strength.*

ISAIAH 40:29 KJV

*Every word of God is flawless;
he is a shield to those who take refuge in him.*

PROVERBS 30:5 NIV

Today's Prayer

Lord, sometimes life is difficult. Sometimes, I am worried, weary, or heartbroken. And sometimes, I encounter powerful temptations to disobey Your commandments. But, when I lift my eyes to You, Father, You strengthen me. When I am weak, You lift me up. Today, I will turn to You for strength, for hope, for direction, and for deliverance.

Amen

Devo 75

Do You Believe in Miracles?

*You are the God who performs miracles;
you display your power among the peoples.*
PSALM 77:14 NIV

D o you believe that God is at work in the world? And do you also believe that nothing is impossible for Him? If so, then you also believe that God is perfectly capable of doing things that you, as a mere human being with limited vision and limited understanding, would deem to be utterly impossible. And that's precisely what God does.

Since the moment that He created our universe out of nothingness, God has made a habit of doing miraculous things. And He still works miracles today. Expect Him to work miracles in your own life, and then be watchful. With God, absolutely nothing is impossible, including an amazing assortment of miracles that He stands ready, willing, and able to perform for you and yours.

Too many Christians live below the miracle level.

VANCE HAVNER

Miracles are not contrary to nature but only contrary
to what we know about nature.

ST. AUGUSTINE

Only God can move mountains,
but faith and prayer can move God.

E. M. BOUNDS

*With God's power working in us, God can do much,
much more than anything we can ask or imagine.*

EPHESIANS 3:20 NCV

*But as it is written: "Eye has not seen, nor ear heard,
nor have entered into the heart of man the things
which God has prepared for those who love Him."*

1 CORINTHIANS 2:9 NKJV

Today's Prayer

Lord, for You nothing is impossible.
Let me trust in Your power to do the
miraculous, and let me trust in Your
willingness to work miracles in my life—
and in my heart.
Amen

Devo 76

Listen Carefully

The one who is from God listens to God's words.
This is why you don't listen, because you are not from God.
JOHN 8:47 HOLMAN CSB

Sometimes God speaks loudly and clearly. More often, He speaks in a quiet voice—and if you are wise, you will be listening carefully when He does. To do so, you must carve out quiet moments each day to study His Word and sense His direction.

Can you quiet yourself long enough to listen to your conscience? Are you attuned to the subtle guidance of your intuition? Are you willing to pray sincerely and then to wait quietly for God's response? Hopefully so. Usually God refrains from sending His messages on stone tablets or city billboards. More often, He communicates in subtler ways. If you sincerely desire to hear His voice, you must listen carefully, and you must do so in the silent corners of your quiet, willing heart.

We cannot experience the fullness of Christ if we do all the expressing. We must allow God to express His love, will, and truth to us.

GARY SMALLEY

In the soul-searching of our lives, we are to stay quiet so we can hear Him say all that He wants to say to us in our hearts.

CHARLES SWINDOLL

Listening is loving.

ZIG ZIGLAR

God has no use for the prayers of the people who won't listen to him.

PROVERBS 28:9 MSG

Trust God from the bottom of your heart; don't try to figure out everything on your own. Listen for God's voice in everything you do, everywhere you go; he's the one who will keep you on track.

PROVERBS 3:5-6 MSG

Listen in silence before me....

—

Isaiah 41:1 NLT

Today's Prayer

Lord, give me the wisdom to be a good listener.
Help me listen carefully to my family,
to my friends, and—
most importantly—to You.
Amen

Devo 77

Big Plans

"I say this because I know what I am planning for you,"
says the Lord. "I have good plans for you, not plans to
hurt you. I will give you hope and a good future."
JEREMIAH 29:11 NCV

Do you think that God has big plans for you, or do you think that God wants you to be a do-nothing Christian? The answer should be obvious, but just for the record, here are the facts: 1. God has plans for your life that are far grander than you can imagine. 2. It's up to you to discover those plans and accomplish them . . . or not.

God has given you many gifts, including the gift of free will; that means that you have the ability to make choices and decisions on your own. The most important decision of your life is, of course, your commitment to accept Jesus Christ as your personal Lord and Savior. And once your eternal destiny is secured, you will undoubtedly ask yourself "What now, Lord?" If you earnestly seek God's plan for your life, you will find it…in time.

Sometimes, God's plans are crystal clear, but other times, He may lead you through the wilderness before He delivers you to the Promised Land. So be patient, keep praying, and keep seeking His will for your life. When you do, you'll be amazed at the marvelous things that an all-powerful, all-knowing God can do.

One of the wonderful things about being a Christian is
the knowledge that God has a plan for our lives.

WARREN WIERSBE

The Almighty does nothing without reason,
although the frail mind of man cannot explain the reason.

ST. AUGUSTINE

Faith never knows where it is being led,
but it loves the One who is leading.

OSWALD CHAMBERS

People may make plans in their minds,
but the Lord decides what they will do.

PROVERBS 16:9 NCV

There is no wisdom, no insight,
no plan that can succeed against the Lord.

PROVERBS 21:30 NIV

Unless the Lord builds a house,
the work of the builders is useless.

PSALM 127:1 NLT

Today's Prayer

Dear Lord, I will seek Your plan for my life. Even when I don't understand why things happen, I will trust You. Even when I am uncertain of my next step, I will trust You. There are many things that I cannot do, Lord, and there are many things that I cannot understand. But one thing I can do is to trust You always. And I will.

Amen

Devo 78

So Laugh!

Laugh with your happy friends when they're happy;
share tears when they're down.
ROMANS 12:15 MSG

Laughter is a gift from God, a gift that He intends for us to use. Yet sometimes, because of the inevitable stresses of everyday living, we fail to find the fun in life. When we allow life's inevitable disappointments to cast a pall over our lives and our souls, we do a profound disservice to ourselves and to our loved ones.

If you've allowed the clouds of life to obscure the blessings of life, perhaps you've formed the unfortunate habit of taking things just a little too seriously. If so, it's time to fret a little less and laugh a little more.

So today, look for the humor that most certainly surrounds you—when you do, you'll find it. And remember: God created laughter for a reason…and Father indeed knows best. So laugh!

If you want people to feel comfortable around you,
to enjoy being with you, then learn to laugh at yourself
and find humor in life's little mishaps.

DENNIS SWANBERG

Laughter is like premium gasoline:
It takes the knock out of living.

ANONYMOUS

I think everybody ought to be a laughing Christian.
I'm convinced that there's just one place where
there's not any laughter, and that's hell.

JERRY CLOWER

Nehemiah said, "Go and enjoy choice food and sweet
drinks, and send some to those who have nothing prepared.
This day is sacred to our Lord. Do not grieve,
for the joy of the LORD is your strength."

NEHEMIAH 8:10 NIV

Clap your hands, all you nations;
shout to God with cries of joy.

PSALM 47:1 NIV

Today's Prayer

Lord, when I begin to take myself or my life too seriously, let me laugh. When I rush from place to place, slow me down, Lord, and let me laugh. Put a smile on my face, Dear Lord, and let me share that smile with all who cross my path . . . and let me laugh.

Amen

Devo 79

Let God judge

Stop judging others, and you will not be judged.
Stop criticizing others, or it will all come back on you.
If you forgive others, you will be forgiven.

LUKE 6:37 NLT

Here's something worth thinking about: If you judge other people harshly, God will judge you in the same fashion. But that's not all (thank goodness!). The Bible also promises that if you forgive others, you, too, will be forgiven. Have you developed the bad habit of behaving yourself like an amateur judge and jury, assigning blame and condemnation wherever you go? If so, it's time to grow up and obey God. When it comes to judging everything and everybody, God doesn't need your help . . . and He doesn't want it.

Christians think they are prosecuting attorneys
or judges, when, in reality,
God has called all of us to be witnesses.

WARREN WIERSBE

An individual Christian may see fit to give up all sorts
of things for special reasons—marriage, or meat,
or beer, or cinema; but the moment he starts saying
these things are bad in themselves, or looking down
his nose at other people who do use them,
he has taken the wrong turn.

C. S. LEWIS

*You, therefore, have no excuse, you who pass judgment
on someone else, for at whatever point you judge
the other, you are condemning yourself.*

ROMANS 2:1 NIV

*Speak and act as those who will be judged by the law of
freedom. For judgment is without mercy to the one who
hasn't shown mercy. Mercy triumphs over judgment.*

JAMES 2:12-13 HOLMAN CSB

Do not judge, or you too will be judged.
For in the same way you judge others,
you will be judged, and with the measure
you use, it will be measured to you.

—

MATTHEW 7:1 NIV

Today's Prayer

Dear Lord, sometimes I am quick to judge
others. But, You have commanded me not to
judge. Keep me mindful, Father, that when
I judge others, I am living outside of Your will
for my life. You have forgiven me, Lord.
Let me forgive others, let me love them,
and let me help them . . .
without judging them.
Amen

Devo 80

You'd Better Beware

Your love must be real. Hate what is evil,
and hold on to what is good.

ROMANS 12:9 NCV

F ace facts: this world is inhabited by quite a few people who are very determined to do evil things. The devil and his human helpers are working 24/7 to cause pain and heartbreak in every corner of the globe . . . including your corner. So you'd better beware.

Your job, if you choose to accept it, is to recognize evil and fight it. The moment that you decide to fight evil whenever you see it, you can no longer be a lukewarm, halfhearted Christian. And, when you are no longer a lukewarm Christian, God rejoices while the devil despairs.

When will you choose to get serious about fighting the evils of our world? Before you answer that question, consider this: in the battle of good versus evil, the devil never takes a day off . . . and neither should you.

God loves you, and He yearns for you to turn away from the path of evil. You need His forgiveness, and you need Him to come into your life and remake you from within.

BILLY GRAHAM

Of two evils, choose neither.

C. H. SPURGEON

Christianity isn't a religion about going to Sunday school, potluck suppers, being nice, holding car washes, sending your secondhand clothes off to Mexico— as good as those things might be. This is a world at war.

JOHN ELDREDGE

For everyone who practices wicked things hates the light and avoids it, so that his deeds may not be exposed. But anyone who lives by the truth comes to the light, so that his works may be shown to be accomplished by God.

JOHN 3:20–21 HOLMAN CSB

He replied, "Every plant that My heavenly Father didn't plant will be uprooted."

MATTHEW 15:13 HOLMAN CSB

The Lord is pleased with a good person,
but he will punish
anyone who plans evil.

—

PROVERBS 12:2 NCV

Today's Prayer

Lord, strengthen my walk with You.
Evil comes in many disguises, and sometimes
it is only with Your help that I can recognize
right from wrong. Your presence in my life
enables me to choose truth and to live
a life pleasing to You. May I always live in
Your presence.

Amen

Devo 81

His Joy and Yours

O clap your hands, all peoples;
Shout to God with the voice of joy.
PSALM 47:1 NASB

Have you made the choice to rejoice? Hopefully so. After all, if you're a believer, you have plenty of reasons to be joyful. Yet sometimes, amid the inevitable hustle and bustle of life-here-on-earth, you may lose sight of your blessings as you wrestle with the challenges of everyday life.

Christ made it clear to His followers: He intended that His joy would become their joy. And it still holds true today: Christ intends that His believers share His love with His joy in their hearts.

What does life have in store for you? A world full of possibilities (of course it's up to you to seize them) and God's promise of abundance (of course it's up to you to accept it). So, as you embark upon the next phase of your journey, remember to celebrate the life that God has given you. Your Creator has blessed you beyond measure. Honor Him with your prayers, your words, your deeds, and your joy.

As Catherine of Siena said,
"All the way to heaven is heaven."
A joyful end requires a joyful means. Bless the Lord.

EUGENE PETERSON

Christ and joy go together.

E. STANLEY JONES

Joy is the serious business of heaven.

C. S. LEWIS

*But now I come to You, and these things I speak in the world,
that they may have My joy fulfilled in themselves.*

JOHN 17:13 NKJV

*Rejoice evermore. Pray without ceasing.
In every thing give thanks: for this is the will of God in Christ
Jesus concerning you.*

1 THESSALONIANS 5:16-18 KJV

Today's Prayer

Dear Lord, You have given me so many blessings; let me celebrate Your gifts. Make me thankful, loving, responsible, and wise. I praise You, Father, for the gift of Your Son and for the priceless gift of salvation. Make me be a joyful Christian and a worthy example to my loved ones, today and every day.

Amen

Devo 82

Imitating Christ

Therefore, be imitators of God, as dearly loved children.
EPHESIANS 5:1 HOLMAN CSB

Imitating Christ is impossible, but attempting to imitate Him is both possible and advisable. By attempting to imitate Jesus, we seek, to the best of our abilities, to walk in His footsteps. To the extent we succeed in following Him, we receive the spiritual abundance that is the rightful possession of those who love Christ and keep His commandments.

Do you seek God's blessings for the day ahead? Then, to the best of your abilities, imitate His Son. You will fall short, of course. But if your heart is right and your intentions are pure, God will bless your efforts, your day, and your life.

A person who gazes and keeps on gazing at Jesus becomes like him in appearance.

E. STANLEY JONES

Christlikeness is not produced by imitation, but by inhabitation.

RICK WARREN

Every Christian is to become a little Christ. The whole purpose of becoming a Christian is simply nothing else.

C. S. LEWIS

But whoever keeps His word, truly the love of God is perfected in him. By this we know that we are in Him. He who says he abides in Him ought himself also to walk just as He walked.

1 JOHN 2:5-6 NKJV

Whoever serves me must follow me. Then my servant will be with me everywhere I am. My Father will honor anyone who serves me.

JOHN 12:26 NCV

Today's Prayer

Dear Jesus, because I am Your disciple,
I will trust You, I will obey Your teachings,
and I will share Your Good News. You have
given me life abundant and life eternal,
and I will follow You today and forever.

Amen

FOR GUYS

The Wisdom to Be Generous

The good person is generous and lends lavishly....
PSALM 112:5 MSG

God's gifts are beyond description, His blessings beyond comprehension. God has been incredibly generous with us, and He rightfully expects us to be generous with others. That's why the thread of generosity is woven into the very fabric of God's teachings.

In the Old Testament, we are told that, "The good person is generous and lends lavishly...." (Psalm 112:5 MSG). And in the New Testament we are instructed, "Freely you have received, freely give" (Matthew 10:8 NKJV). These principles still apply. As we establish priorities for our days and our lives, we are advised to give freely of our time, our possessions, and our love—just as God has given freely to us.

Of course, we can never fully repay God for His gifts, but we can share them with others. And we should.

If you want to be truly happy, you won't find it on
an endless quest for more stuff. You'll find it in receiving
God's generosity and then passing that generosity along.

BILL HYBELS

Nothing is really ours until we share it.

C. S. LEWIS

We are never more like God than when we give.

CHARLES SWINDOLL

So let each one give as he purposes in his heart,
not grudgingly or of necessity;
for God loves a cheerful giver.

2 CORINTHIANS 9:7 NKJV

Dear friend, you are showing your faith
by whatever you do for the brothers,
and this you are doing for strangers.

3 JOHN 1:5 HOLMAN CSB

Bear one another's burdens,
and so fulfill the law of Christ.

GALATIANS 6:2 NKJV

Today's Prayer

Lord, You have been so generous with me;
let me be generous with others.
Help me to give generously of my time
and my possessions as I care for those in need.
And, make me a humble giver, Lord, so that all
the glory and the praise might be Yours.
Amen

Beyond Guilt

There is therefore now no condemnation to those who are in Christ Jesus, who do not walk according to the flesh, but according to the Spirit.

ROMANS 8:1 NKJV

All of us have made mistakes. Sometimes our failures result from our own shortsightedness. On other occasions, we are swept up in events that are beyond our abilities to control. Under either set of circumstances, we may experience intense feelings of guilt. But God has an answer for the guilt that we feel. That answer, of course, is His forgiveness.

When we ask our Heavenly Father for His forgiveness, He forgives us completely and without reservation. Then, we must do the difficult work of forgiving ourselves in the same way that God has forgiven us: thoroughly and unconditionally.

If you're feeling guilty, then it's time for a special kind of housecleaning—a housecleaning of your mind and your heart . . . beginning NOW!

Prayer is essential when a believer is
stuck in the pits of unresolved guilt.

CHARLES STANLEY

Guilt is a gift that leads us to grace.

FRANKLIN GRAHAM

Identify the sin. Confess it. Turn from it.
Avoid it at all costs. Live with a clean, forgiven conscience.
Don't dwell on what God has forgotten!

MAX LUCADO

*Your beliefs about these things should be kept secret
between you and God. People are happy if they can do
what they think is right without feeling guilty.*

ROMANS 14:22 NCV

*Be diligent to present yourself approved to God,
a worker who doesn't need to be ashamed,
correctly teaching the word of truth.*

2 TIMOTHY 2:15 HOLMAN CSB

Today's Prayer

Dear Lord, thank You for the guilt that
I feel when I disobey You. Help me confess
my wrongdoings, help me accept
Your forgiveness, and help me renew
my passion to serve You.

Amen

Devo 85

Beyond Mistakes

*Instead, God has chosen the world's foolish things
to shame the wise, and God has chosen
the world's weak things to shame the strong.*

1 CORINTHIANS 1:27 HOLMAN CSB

Mistakes: nobody likes 'em but everybody makes 'em. Sometimes, even if you're a very good person, you're going to mess things up. And when you do, God is always ready to forgive you—He'll do His part, but you should be willing to do your part, too. Here's what you need to do:

1. If you've been engaging in behavior that is against the will of God, cease and desist (that means stop). 2. If you made a mistake, learn from it and don't repeat it (that's called getting smarter). 3. If you've hurt somebody, apologize and ask for forgiveness (that's called doing the right thing). 4. Ask for God's forgiveness, too (He'll give it whenever you ask, but you do need to ask!). Have you made a mistake? If so, today is the perfect day to make things right with everybody (and the word "everybody" includes yourself, your family, your friends, and your God).

Mistakes are the price you pay for being human; repeated mistakes are the price you pay for being stubborn. So don't be hardheaded: learn from your experiences—the first time!

I hope you don't mind me telling you all this.
One can learn only by seeing one's mistakes.

C. S. LEWIS

Truth will sooner come out of error than from confusion.

FRANCIS BACON

Lord, when we are wrong, make us willing to change;
and when we are right, make us easy to live with.

PETER MARSHALL

*If we confess our sins to him, he is faithful
and just to forgive us and to cleanse us from every wrong.*

1 JOHN 1:9 NLT

*Have mercy on me, O God, according to your unfailing love;
according to your great compassion blot out
my transgressions. Wash away all my iniquity
and cleanse me from my sin.*

PSALM 51:1-2 NIV

Today's Prayer

Dear Lord, there's a right way to do things
and a wrong way to do things.
When I do things that are wrong, help me be
quick to ask for forgiveness . . .
and quick to correct my mistakes.
Amen

Devo 86

God's Guidance

Every morning he wakes me. He teaches me to listen like a student. The Lord God helps me learn...
ISAIAH 50:4-5 NCV

The Bible promises that God will guide you if you let Him. Your job, of course, is to let Him. But sometimes, you will be tempted to do otherwise. Sometimes, you'll be tempted to go along with the crowd; other times, you'll be tempted to do things your way, not God's way. When you feel those temptations, resist them.

What will you allow to guide you through the coming day: your own desires (or, for that matter, the desires of your friends)? Or will you allow God to lead the way? The answer should be obvious. You should let God be your guide. When you entrust your life to Him completely and without reservation, God will give you the strength to meet any challenge, the courage to face any trial, and the wisdom to live in His righteousness. So trust Him today and seek His guidance. When you do, your next step will be the right one.

We must always invite Jesus to be the navigator
of our plans, desires, wills, and emotions,
for He is the way, the truth, and the life.

BILL BRIGHT

Fix your eyes upon the Lord! Do it once.
Do it daily. Do it constantly.
Look at the Lord and keep looking at Him.

CHARLES SWINDOLL

God's plan for our guidance is for us to grow gradually in
wisdom before we get to the crossroads.

BILL HYBELS

Lord, You light my lamp; my God illuminates my darkness.

PSALM 18:28 HOLMAN CSB

*In all your ways acknowledge Him,
and He shall direct your paths.*

PROVERBS 3:6 NKJV

The true children of God are those
who let God's Spirit lead them.

ROMANS 8:14 NCV

Today's Prayer

Dear Lord, thank You for Your constant presence and Your constant love. I draw near to You this day with the confidence that You are ready to guide me. Help me walk closely with You, Father, and help me share Your Good News with all who cross my path.

Amen

Devo 87

Getting It Done Now

When you make a vow to God, don't delay fulfilling it, because He does not delight in fools. Fulfill what you vow.

ECCLESIASTES 5:4 HOLMAN CSB

When something important needs to be done, the best time to do it is sooner rather than later. But sometimes, instead of doing the smart thing (which, by the way, is choosing "sooner"), we may choose "later." When we do, we may pay a heavy price for our shortsightedness.

Are you one of those people who puts things off till the last minute? If so, it's time to change your ways. Your procrastination is probably the result of your shortsighted attempt to postpone (or avoid altogether) the discomfort that you associate with a particular activity. Get over it!

Whatever "it" is, do it now. When you do, you won't have to worry about "it" later.

Every time you refuse to face up to life and its problems,
you weaken your character.

E. STANLEY JONES

Do noble things, do not dream them all day long.

CHARLES KINGSLEY

Now is the only time worth having because,
indeed, it is the only time we have.

C. H. SPURGEON

*For the Kingdom of God is not just fancy talk;
it is living by God's power.*

1 CORINTHIANS 4:20 NLT

*Therefore, get your minds ready for action,
being self-disciplined, and set your hope completely
on the grace to be brought to you
at the revelation of Jesus Christ.*

1 PETER 1:13 HOLMAN CSB

But prove yourselves doers of the word,
and not merely hearers.

—

JAMES 1:22 NASB

Today's Prayer

Dear Lord, today is a new day.
Help me tackle the important tasks
immediately, even if those tasks are
unpleasant. Don't let me put off until
tomorrow what I should do today.

Amen

Devo 88

The Dating Game

Do not be unequally yoked together with unbelievers.
For what fellowship has righteousness with lawlessness?
And what communion has light with darkness?

2 CORINTHIANS 6:14 NKJV

Oh, how glorious are the dreams of love—but oh how tough it is to turn those dreams into reality! If you're still searching for Miss Right, be patient, be prudent, and be picky. Look for a girl whose values you respect, whose behavior you approve of, and whose faith you admire. Remember that appearances can be deceiving and tempting, so watch your step. And when it comes to the important task of building a lifetime relationship with the girl of your dreams, pray about it! God is waiting to give His approval—or not—but He won't give it until He's asked. So ask, listen, and decide accordingly.

What really builds togetherness is time spent together—
lots of time.

DENNIS SWANBERG

We discover our role in life through our relationships
with others.

RICK WARREN

I don't buy the cliché that quality time is the most
important thing. If you don't have enough quantity,
you won't get quality.

LEIGHTON FORD

*Be sober! Be on the alert! Your adversary
the Devil is prowling around like a roaring lion,
looking for anyone he can devour.*

1 PETER 5:8 HOLMAN CSB

*Light shines on the godly, and joy on those who do right.
May all who are godly be happy in the Lord
and praise his holy name.*

PSALM 97:11-12 NLT

Today's Prayer

Lord, I will let You rule over every aspect
of my life, including my relationships.
And I know that when I do, You will help me
make choices that are right for me,
today and every day that I live.
Amen

When You Have Doubts

An indecisive man is unstable in all his ways.

JAMES 1:8 HOLMAN CSB

If you've never had any doubts about your faith, then you can stop reading this page now and skip to the next. But if you've ever been plagued by doubts about your faith or your God, keep reading.

Even some of the most faithful Christians are, at times, beset by occasional bouts of discouragement and doubt. But even when we feel far removed from God, God is never far removed from us. He is always with us, always willing to calm the storms of life—always willing to replace our doubts with comfort and assurance.

Whenever you're plagued by doubts, that's precisely the moment you should seek God's presence by genuinely seeking to establish a deeper, more meaningful relationship with His Son. Then you may rest assured that in time, God will calm your fears, answer your prayers, and restore your confidence.

There is a difference between doubt and unbelief. Doubt is a matter of mind: we cannot understand what God is doing or why He is doing it. Unbelief is a matter of will: we refuse to believe God's Word and obey what He tells us to do.

WARREN WIERSBE

We basically have two choices to make in dealing with the mysteries of God. We can wrestle with Him or we can rest in Him.

CALVIN MILLER

When doubts filled my mind,
your comfort gave me renewed hope and cheer.
PSALM 94:19 NLT

Jesus said, "Because you have seen Me,
you have believed. Blessed are those
who believe without seeing."
JOHN 20:29 HOLMAN CSB

Today's Prayer

Dear God, sometimes this world can be
a puzzling place, filled with uncertainty and
doubt. When I am unsure of my next step, keep
me mindful that You are always near and that
You can overcome any challenge.
Give me faith, Father, and let me remember
always that with Your love and Your power,
I can live courageously and faithfully
today and every day.
Amen

Devo 90

Love According to God

This is my command: Love one another the way I loved you.
This is the very best way to love.
Put your life on the line for your friends.
JOHN 15:12-13 MSG

Love, like everything else in this wonderful world, begins and ends with God, but the middle part belongs to us. God has given each of us the opportunity to become a loving person—or not. God has given each of us the opportunity to be kind, to be courteous, to be cooperative, and to be forgiving—or not. God has given each of us the chance to obey the Golden Rule, or to make up our own rules as we go. If we obey God's rules, we're safe, but if we do otherwise, we're headed for trouble in a hurry.

God does not intend for you to experience mediocre relationships; He created you for far greater things. Building lasting relationships requires compassion, wisdom, empathy, kindness, courtesy, and forgiveness. If that sounds a lot like work, it is—which is perfectly fine with God. Why? Because He knows that you are capable of doing that work, and because He knows that the fruits of your labors will enrich the lives of your loved ones and the lives of generations yet unborn.

How do you spell love? When you reach the point where the happiness, security, and development of another person is as much of a driving force to you as your own happiness, security, and development, then you have a mature love. True love is spelled G-I-V-E. It is not based on what you can get, but rooted in what you can give to the other person.

JOSH MCDOWELL

Love is not grabbing or self-centered or selfish. Real love is being able to contribute to the happiness of another person without expecting to get anything in return.

JAMES DOBSON

If I speak the languages of men and of angels, but do not have love, I am a sounding gong or a clanging cymbal.

1 CORINTHIANS 13:1 HOLMAN CSB

Dear friends, if God loved us in this way, we also must love one another.

1 JOHN 4:11 HOLMAN CSB

Hatred stirs up conflicts,
but love covers all offenses.

—

PROVERBS 10:12 HCSB

Today's Prayer

Lord, You have given me the gift of eternal love; let me share that gift with the world. Help me, Father, to show kindness to those who cross my path, and let me show tenderness and unfailing love to my family and friends. Make me generous with words of encouragement and praise. And, help me always to reflect the love that Christ Jesus gave me so that through me, others might find Him.

Amen

Devo 91

The Gift of Eternal Life

*Just then someone came up and asked Him, "Teacher,
what good must I do to have eternal life?" "Why do you ask
Me about what is good?" He said to him. "There is only
One who is good. If you want to enter into life,
keep the commandments."*

MATTHEW 19:16-17 HOLMAN CSB

Your ability to envision the future, like your life here
on earth, is limited. God's vision, however, is not
burdened by any such limitations. He sees all things,
He knows all things, and His plans for you endure for all
time.

God's plans are not limited to the events of life-here-
on-earth. Your Heavenly Father has bigger things in mind
for you . . . much bigger things. So praise the Creator for
the gift of eternal life and share the Good News with all
who cross your path. You have given your heart to the Son,
so you belong to the Father—today, tomorrow, and for all
eternity.

Teach us to set our hopes on heaven,
to hold firmly to the promise of eternal life, so that we can
withstand the struggles and storms of this world.

MAX LUCADO

That which is born of the flesh may die.
That which is born of the Spirit shall live forever.

D. L. MOODY

God loves you and wants you to experience peace
and life—abundant and eternal.

BILLY GRAHAM

*And this is the testimony: that God has given us eternal life,
and this life is in His Son. He who has the Son has life;
he who does not have the Son of God does not have life.*

1 JOHN 5:11-12 NKJV

*And this is the will of Him who sent Me, that everyone who
sees the Son and believes in Him may have everlasting life;
and I will raise him up at the last day.*

JOHN 6:40 NKJV

These things I have written to you who
believe in the name of the Son of God,
that you may know that you
have eternal life.

1 JOHN 5:13 NKJV

Today's Prayer

Lord, I am only here on this earth for a brief while. But, You have offered me the priceless gift of eternal life through Your Son Jesus. I accept Your gift, Lord, with thanksgiving and praise. Let me share the good news of my salvation with those who need Your healing touch.

Amen

Devo 92

Finding Hope

*This hope we have as an anchor of the soul,
a hope both sure and steadfast.*
HEBREWS 6:19 NASB

There are few sadder sights on earth than the sight of a girl or guy who has lost hope. In difficult times, hope can be elusive, but those who place their faith in God's promises need never lose it. After all, God is good; His love endures; He has promised His children the gift of eternal life. And, God keeps His promises.

If you find yourself falling into the spiritual traps of worry and discouragement, seek the healing touch of Jesus and the encouraging words of fellow believers. And if you find a friend in need, remind him or her of the peace that is found through a genuine relationship with Christ. It was Christ who promised, "I have told you these things so that in Me you may have peace. In the world you have suffering. But take courage! I have conquered the world" (John 16:33 Holman CSB). This world can be a place of trials and troubles, but as believers, we are secure. God has promised us peace, joy, and eternal life. And, of course, God keeps His promises today, tomorrow, and forever.

The hope we have in Jesus is the anchor for the soul—
something sure and steadfast, preventing drifting
or giving way, lowered to the depth of God's love.

FRANKLIN GRAHAM

Faith looks back and draws courage;
hope looks ahead and keeps desire alive.

JOHN ELDREDGE

If your hopes are being disappointed just now,
it means that they are being purified.

OSWALD CHAMBERS

*Let us hold on to the confession of our hope without
wavering, for He who promised is faithful.*

HEBREWS 10:23 HOLMAN CSB

*May the God of hope fill you with all joy and peace as you
trust in him, so that you may overflow with hope
by the power of the Holy Spirit.*

ROMANS 15:13 NIV

Sustain me as You promised,
and I will live;
do not let me be ashamed of my hope.

—

PSALM 119:116 HCSB

Today's Prayer

Today, Dear Lord, I will live in hope.
If I become discouraged, I will turn to You.
If I grow weary, I will seek strength in You.
In every aspect of my life, I will trust You.
You are my Father, Lord, and I place
my hope and my faith in You.
Amen

Devo 93

The Best Policy

*Better to be poor and honest than
a rich person no one can trust.*

PROVERBS 19:1 MSG

t has been said on many occasions and in many ways that honesty is the best policy. For believers, it is far more important to note that honesty is God's policy. And if we are to be servants worthy of our Savior, Jesus Christ, we must be honest and forthright in our communications with others.

Sometimes, honesty is difficult; sometimes, honesty is painful; always, honesty is God's commandment. In the Book of Exodus, God did not command, "Thou shalt not bear false witness when it is convenient." And He didn't say, "Thou shalt not bear false witness most of the time." God said, "Thou shalt not bear false witness against thy neighbor." Period.

Sometime soon, perhaps even today, you will be tempted to bend the truth or perhaps even to break it. Resist that temptation. Truth is God's way…and it must also be yours. Period.

A little lie is like a little pregnancy.
It doesn't take long before everyone knows.

C. S. Lewis

Integrity is not a given factor in everyone's life.
It is a result of self-discipline, inner trust,
and a decision to be relentlessly honest
in all situations in our lives.

John Maxwell

God doesn't expect you to be perfect,
but he does insist on complete honesty.

Rick Warren

Ye shall not steal, neither deal falsely,
neither lie one to another.

Leviticus 19:11 KJV

So put away all falsehood and "tell your neighbor the truth"
because we belong to each other.

Ephesians 4:25 NLT

Today's Prayer

Heavenly Father, You instruct Your children
to seek truth and to live righteously.
Help me always to live according to Your
commandments. Sometimes, Lord, speaking
the truth is difficult, but let me always speak
truthfully and forthrightly. And, let me walk
righteously and courageously so that others
might see Your grace reflected
in my words and my deeds.
Amen

Devo 94

Healthy Habits

Do not be deceived: "Evil company corrupts good habits."
1 CORINTHIANS 15:33 NKJV

It's an old saying and a true one: First, you make your habits, and then your habits make you. Some habits will inevitably bring you closer to God; other habits will lead you away from the path He has chosen for you. If you sincerely desire to improve your spiritual health, you must honestly examine the habits that make up the fabric of your day. And you must abandon those habits that are displeasing to God.

If you trust God, and if you keep asking for His help, He can transform your life. If you sincerely ask Him to help you, the same God who created the universe will help you defeat the harmful habits that have heretofore defeated you. So, if at first you don't succeed, keep praying. God is listening, and He's ready to help you become a better person if you ask Him . . . so ask today.

Since behaviors become habits,
make them work with you and not against you.

E. STANLEY JONES

You will never change your life until you change
something you do daily.

JOHN MAXWELL

The simple fact is that if we sow a lifestyle that is in
direct disobedience to God's reveled Word,
we ultimately reap disaster.

CHARLES SWINDOLL

*Dear friend, I pray that you may prosper in every way
and be in good health, just as your soul prospers.*

3 JOHN 1:2 HOLMAN CSB

*Therefore, brothers, by the mercies of God,
I urge you to present your bodies as a living sacrifice,
holy and pleasing to God; this is your spiritual worship.*

ROMANS 12:1 HOLMAN CSB

Today's Prayer

Dear Lord, help me break bad habits
and form good ones. And let my actions
be pleasing to You, today and every day.

Amen

Devo 95

Swing Away!

Let us not become weary in doing good, for at the proper
time we will reap a harvest if we do not give up.

GALATIANS 6:9 NIV

His adoring fans called him the "Sultan of Swat." He was Babe Ruth, the baseball player who set records for home runs and strikeouts. Babe's philosophy was simple. He said, "Never let the fear of striking out get in your way." That's smart advice on the diamond or off.

Of course it's never wise to take foolish risks (so buckle up, slow down, and don't do anything stupid!). But when it comes to the game of life, you should not let the fear of failure keep you from taking your swings.

Today, ask God for the courage to step beyond the boundaries of your self-doubts. Ask Him to guide you to a place where you can realize your full potential—a place where you are freed from the fear of failure. Ask Him to do His part, and promise Him that you will do your part. Don't ask Him to lead you to a "safe" place; ask Him to lead you to the "right" place . . . and remember: those two places are seldom the same.

If you learn from a defeat, you have not really lost.

ZIG ZIGLAR

No matter how badly we have failed,
we can always get up and begin again.
Our God is the God of new beginnings.

WARREN WIERSBE

Success or failure can be pretty well predicted
by the degree to which the heart is fully in it.

JOHN ELDREDGE

*If we confess our sins to him, he is faithful and just to forgive
us and to cleanse us from every wrong.*

1 JOHN 1:9 NLT

*If you hide your sins, you will not succeed.
If you confess and reject them, you will receive mercy.*

PROVERBS 28:13 NCV

*If you listen to constructive criticism,
you will be at home among the wise.*

PROVERBS 15:31 NLT

If you listen to constructive criticism,
you will be at home among the wise.

PROVERBS 15:31 NLT

Today's Prayer

Dear Lord, even when I'm afraid of failure, give me the courage to try. Remind me that with You by my side, I really have nothing to fear. So today, Father, I will live courageously as I place my faith in You.

Amen

Devo 96

Richly Blessed

*The Lord bless you and protect you; the Lord make His face
shine on you, and be gracious to you.*

Numbers 6:24-25 Holman CSB

Have you counted your blessings lately? If you
sincerely wish to follow in Christ's footsteps, you
should make thanksgiving a habit, a regular part of
your daily routine.

How has God blessed you? First and foremost, He has
given you the gift of eternal life through the sacrifice of
His only begotten Son, but the blessings don't stop there.
Today, take time to make a partial list of God's gifts to
you: the talents, the opportunities, the possessions, and the
relationships that you may, on occasion, take for granted.
And then, when you've spent sufficient time listing your
blessings, offer a prayer of gratitude to the Giver of all things
good . . . and, to the best of your ability, use your gifts for
the glory of His kingdom.

It is when we give ourselves to be a blessing that we can specially count on the blessing of God.

ANDREW MURRAY

We prevent God from giving us the great spiritual gifts He has in store for us, because we do not give thanks for daily gifts.

DIETRICH BONHOEFFER

God's love for His children is unconditional, no strings attached. But, God's blessings on our lives do come with a condition—obedience. If we are to receive the fullness of God's blessings, we must obey Him and keep His commandments.

JIM GALLERY

I will make them and the area around My hill a blessing: I will send down showers in their season— showers of blessing.

EZEKIEL 34:26 HOLMAN CSB

The Lord bless you and keep you; The Lord make His face shine upon you, And be gracious to you.

NUMBERS 6:24-25 NKJV

Blessed is a man who endures trials,
because when he passes the test he will
receive the crown of life that He has
promised to those who love Him.

—

James 1:12 HCSB

Today's Prayer

Today, Lord, let me count my blessings
with thanksgiving in my heart. You have
cared for me, Lord, and I will give You the glory
and the praise. Let me accept Your blessings
and Your gifts, and let me share them
with others, just as You first shared
them with me.

Amen

Devo 97

God's Timetable

He has made everything beautiful in its time.
He has also set eternity in the hearts of men;
yet they cannot fathom what God has done
from beginning to end.

ECCLESIASTES 3:11 NIV

Are you anxious for God to work out His plan for your life? Who isn't? As believers, we all want God to do great things for us and through us, and we want Him to do those things now. But sometimes, God has other plans. Sometimes, God's timetable does not coincide with our own. It's worth noting, however, that God's timetable is always perfect.

The next time you find your patience tested to the limit, remember that the world unfolds according to God's plan, not ours. Sometimes, we must wait patiently, and that's as it should be. After all, think how patient God has been with us.

God is in no hurry. Compared to the works of mankind,
He is extremely deliberate.
God is not a slave to the human clock.

CHARLES SWINDOLL

God has a designated time when his promise
will be fulfilled and the prayer will be answered.

JIM CYMBALA

Will not the Lord's time be better than your time?

C. H. SPURGEON

*Humble yourselves, therefore, under God's mighty hand,
that he may lift you up in due time.*

1 PETER 5:6 NIV

*From one man he made every nation of men,
that they should inhabit the whole earth;
and he determined the times set for them and the exact
places where they should live.*

ACTS 17:26 NIV

Wait for the LORD; be strong
and take heart and wait for the LORD.

—

Psalm 27:14 NIV

Today's Prayer

Dear Lord, Your wisdom is infinite,
and the timing of Your heavenly plan is
perfect. You have a plan for my life that is
grander than I can imagine. When I am
impatient, remind me that You are never early
or late. You are always on time, Father,
so let me trust in You.

Amen

Devo 98

His Disciple

He has showed you, O man, what is good.
And what does the LORD require of you? To act justly
and to love mercy and to walk humbly with your God.
MICAH 6:8 NIV

When Jesus addressed His disciples, He warned that each one must, "take up his cross and follow me." The disciples must have known exactly what the Master meant. In Jesus' day, prisoners were forced to carry their own crosses to the location where they would be put to death. Thus, Christ's message was clear: in order to follow Him, Christ's disciples must deny themselves and, instead, trust Him completely. Nothing has changed since then.

If we are to be disciples of Christ, we must trust Him and place Him at the very center of our beings. Jesus never comes "next." He is always first. The paradox, of course, is that only by sacrificing ourselves to Him do we gain salvation for ourselves.

Do you seek to be a worthy disciple of Christ? Then pick up His cross today and every day that you live. When you do, He will bless you now and forever.

A disciple is a follower of Christ. That means you take on His priorities as your own. His agenda becomes your agenda. His mission becomes your mission.

CHARLES STANLEY

As we seek to become disciples of Jesus Christ, we should never forget that the word disciple is directly related to the word discipline. To be a disciple of the Lord Jesus Christ is to know his discipline.

DENNIS SWANBERG

There is no Christianity without a cross, for you cannot be a disciple of Jesus without taking up your cross.

HENRY BLACKABY

"Follow Me," Jesus told them, "and I will make you into fishers of men!" Immediately they left their nets and followed Him.

MARK 1:17-18 HCSB

Be imitators of God, therefore, as dearly loved children.

EPHESIANS 5:1 NIV

"While you have the light,
believe in the light,
that you may become sons of light."
These things Jesus spoke, and departed,
and was hidden from them.

JOHN 12:36 NKJV

Today's Prayer

Help me, Lord, to understand what cross I am
to bear this day. Give me the strength and
the courage to carry that cross along the path
of Your choosing so that I may be
a worthy disciple of Your Son.
Amen

Devo 99

Wisdom Now!

*Do you want to be counted wise, to build a reputation
for wisdom? Here's what you do:
Live well, live wisely, live humbly. It's the way you live,
not the way you talk, that counts.*

JAMES 3:13 MSG

Are you a wise guy? Hopefully, you're a very wise fellow who's getting wiser every day. But even if you're a very smart fellow, there's still lots more for you to learn.

Wisdom is not like a dandelion or a mushroom; it does not spring up overnight. It is, instead, like an oak tree that starts as a tiny acorn, grows into a sapling, and eventually reaches up to the sky, tall and strong. To become wise, you must seek God's wisdom and live according to His Word. To become wise, you must seek wisdom with consistency and purpose. To become wise, you must not only learn the lessons of the Christian life, you must also live by them.

Are you passionate in your pursuit of God's wisdom? And do you sincerely seek to live a life of righteousness? If so, you must study the ultimate source of wisdom: the Word of God. You must seek out worthy teachers and listen carefully to their advice. You must associate, day in and day out, with godly friends. And, you must act in accordance with your beliefs. When you do these things, you will become wise . . . and you will be a blessing to your friends, to your family, and to the world.

If you lack knowledge, go to school.
If you lack wisdom, get on your knees.

VANCE HAVNER

The more wisdom enters our hearts, the more we will be
able to trust our hearts in difficult situations.

JOHN ELDREDGE

Don't expect wisdom to come into your life like great chunks
of rock on a conveyor belt. Wisdom comes privately
from God as a byproduct of right decisions,
godly reactions, and the application of
spiritual principles to daily circumstances.

CHARLES SWINDOLL

*The Lord says, "I will make you wise and show you
where to go. I will guide you and watch over you."*
PSALM 32:8 NCV

*Wisdom is the principal thing; therefore get wisdom.
And in all your getting, get understanding.*
PROVERBS 4:7 NKJV

Today's Prayer

Dear Lord, when I trust in the wisdom
of the world, I am often led astray, but when
I trust in Your wisdom, I build my life upon
a firm foundation. Today and every day
I will trust Your Word and follow it, knowing
that the ultimate wisdom is Your wisdom
and the ultimate truth is Your truth.

Amen

Devo 100

How Much Love?

His banner over me was love.

SONG OF SOLOMON 2:4 KJV

How much does God love you? As long as you're alive, you'll never be able to figure it out because God's love is just too big to comprehend. But this much we know: God loves you so much that He sent His Son Jesus to come to this earth and to die for you! And, when you accepted Jesus into your heart, God gave you a gift that is more precious than gold: the gift of eternal life.

God's love is bigger and more powerful than anybody can imagine, but His love is very real. So do yourself a favor right now: accept God's love with open arms and welcome His Son Jesus into your heart. When you do, your life will be changed today, tomorrow, and forever.

God wants to emancipate his people; he wants to set them
free. He wants his people to be not slaves but sons.
He wants them governed not by law but by love.

MAX LUCADO

The hope we have in Jesus is the anchor for the soul—
something sure and steadfast, preventing drifting
or giving way, lowered to the depth of God's love.

FRANKLIN GRAHAM

He is the same yesterday, today, and forever,
and His unchanging and unfailing love sustains me
when nothing and no one else can.

BILL BRIGHT

*We know how much God loves us, and we have put
our trust in him. God is love, and all who live in love
live in God, and God lives in them.*

1 JOHN 4:16 NLT

*As the Father loved Me, I also have loved you;
abide in My love.*

JOHN 15:9 NKJV

Whoever is wise will observe these things,
and they will understand
the lovingkindness of the Lord.

—

PSALM 107:43 NKJV

Today's Prayer

Dear Lord, the Bible tells me that You
are my loving Father. I thank You, Lord,
for Your love and for Your Son.
Amen

Notes and Favorite Scripture

Use the following pages to jot down your thoughts, ideas, and favorite Scripture.

FOR GUYS